Successful Personal Statements to Get You into a Top University

Successful Personal Statements to Get You into a Top University

Edited by Warren Zhang and
Hemant Mohapatra

Constable & Robinson Ltd
55–56 Russell Square
London WC1B 4HP
www.constablerobinson.com

First published in the UK by How To Books,
an imprint of Constable & Robinson Ltd, 2014

A copy of the British Library Cataloguing in Publication
Data is available from the British Library

ISBN 978-1-84528-514-2 (trade paperback)
ISBN 978-1-47211-016-9 (ebook)

Printed and bound in the UK
by CPI Group (UK) Ltd, Croydon, CR0 4YY

1 3 5 7 9 10 8 6 4 2

Contents

Acknowledgements

We are extremely grateful to the students at Cambridge University for their time, effort and trust in us to submit their Personal Statements to be included in this book. The submissions we received far exceeded our expectations in terms of quality, quantity and diversity. We would also like to thank the final fifty contributors to the book; without them, this project would not have been possible.

We are indebted to our co-editors – Anna Claeys, Gwen Jing and Arjun Sajip, Cambridge University students involved with various university newspapers in editorial or journalistic capacities – for their outstanding analysis, effort and quality of work, which has added a new dimension to our publication.

Our thanks further extend to Nikki Read and Giles Lewis at How To Books and the team at Constable & Robinson for their help, guidance and trust in us to write this book.

Huge thanks to Daniel Gulati, Harvard Business School alumnus and author of *Passion and Purpose*, Harvard Business Review Press (2011), and Dr Mark De Rond, professor at University of Cambridge Judge Business School and author of the bestseller *There Is an I in Team*, Harvard Business Review Press (2012), for their guidance and advice in formulating our book proposal. It was our initial discussions with Daniel and Dr De Rond that helped structure our vision for the book and forced us to think critically about the larger mission we are trying to accomplish – giving everyone an equal footing to compete for a place at some of the top universities worldwide.

Preface

In 2011, over 580,000 students competed fiercely for limited university places at leading UK universities where acceptance rates are less than 20 per cent. Places at top educational institutions are highly competitive and selective, and all students are looking for an edge. This book will help prospective candidates answer a very specific question: what makes for a successful Personal Statement?

The content of this book will have a broad appeal to prospective university students applying to universities in the UK and abroad. It is meant for anyone wishing to apply for an undergraduate course at a university that requires writing a sample and/or a statement of purpose. Tutors, advisers and parents who are looking to provide candidates with university subject advice, plan future careers and consult on meeting admissions criteria will also find this book a useful tool.

We would like to point out that the views and opinions expressed in the book do not reflect those of the University of Cambridge, nor are they officially endorsed by its admissions committee(s). Reading this book does not guarantee admission into any university but, used judiciously, it should help students put together a more thoughtful, honest and holistic package when compiling an application to a university.

Our goal is to highlight personal statements of the highest standard from students at Cambridge University to set a benchmark of success, and to offer practical ways of improving your own Personal Statement to gain admission to the university of your choice. Throughout the book, we'll also discover that there is no right or wrong approach to writing a strong Personal Statement. What truly matters is that your Personal Statement shows depth of self-awareness, passion and a clear path to your future goals, and then goes on to explain how studying at a university will help you achieve those goals.

Part I

Applying to a Top University

1

Why Study at a Top University?

Most common reasons

Going to university is tough. It takes time, energy and, let's not forget, money! So why do so many people spend a majority of their teenage years working hard so they can get into a top university, only to work harder again?

The answer is simple: university is the gateway to opportunity. It is that one, undeniable, stamp of approval that endorses your intelligence, persistence and fortitude. Sure, there are many who have gone on to do great things without a university education, but the number of people who have done so is extremely low. In the bestselling book by Nassim Nicholas Taleb, *The Black Swan*, you may come to realize just how lucky many of our society's high achievers are. Universities tend to 'normalize' our luck. Opportunities are useful only when you are ready for them. Studying at a university increases your chances more than almost anything else to prepare you for life's major opportunities.

In going through some of the Personal Statements from the university graduates we interviewed, you will notice that people tend to go to universities for a variety of reasons – some personal, some professional:

> *I went to Imperial because it is in the heart of London, the gateway to Europe and a place I always wanted to live. Imperial is consistently ranked in the Top 20 universities in the world and has a great reputation for science and engineering. As an aspiring engineer, it is the ideal place for me to gain the knowledge for my future career.*
>
> Ralph Qiu, Imperial College (Bachelor of Material Engineering)

> *As an Asian-American student studying in the US, I wasn't aware that not going to university was an option.*
>
> Elaine Chow, New York University (Bachelor of Journalism)

> *College was never really a question, always wanted to go. I actually enjoyed studying and learning. As for where I went, I wanted to go somewhere that I could gain some independence from my parents (thus distance from Florida)*

and I wanted to go to a well-ranked school. Since I had a scholarship from the Army, I also needed to find a school that had an Army ROTC program.

Ruthie Levy, Cornell University (Bachelor of Science, US Army)

[I went to college because] I recognized the financial and intellectual value of a college education, and also to challenge myself personally.

John Wingfield-Hill, King's College London
(Bachelor of Science in Physics)

Benefits

We believe there are four major benefits to attending a top university: branding, network, skills and financial outcomes.

Branding

Universities with the strongest brands attract the highest-calibre students – these are individuals who are already programmed for success because they are hard-working, smart and learn quickly from their failures. We have been conditioned to believe that a student who has attended a university (or, in some cases, a top university) is more likely to succeed. In some ways, it's a self-fulfilling prophesy, too; opportunities open up for them more easily, and those very opportunities are seen as some measure of 'success'.

So, having that brand on your résumé is definitely going to help you get noticed more easily; in our overcrowded job market, sometimes that's the biggest hurdle. And it is no secret that all employers use 'signals' to narrow down the number of candidates they think would succeed in their advertised roles. One of the signals they use is university education. The more educated you are, the stronger the signal you send to the employer of your employability. Indeed, it also follows that the more renowned and the higher regarded your university is, the stronger the signal.

Network

For most of us, university is the place we will make the strongest bonds with our friends, partners and colleagues. This network of people we create at university is going to be one of the most important, and one shouldn't underestimate its value. Whether you are planning to enter the corporate world, start a firm of your own or enter academia, this network, if developed honestly and carefully, will serve you well. Some of the most famous companies in the world – including Google and Facebook – were co-founded by people who met and became close friends while attending university.

University is full of countless opportunities for networking and building your circle of friends by providing opportunities to become involved in (or lead) the numerous organizations and clubs that add value to the student community on campus. The list of people who were actively involved in serving the student community, and who later went on to become CEOs or even leading statesmen and women, is a long list indeed. For example, US president Barack Obama was the first black president of the *Harvard Law Review* while he was a student at the Harvard Law School in 1988. Getting involved in these roles allows one to make new connections which might lead to interesting and highly productive opportunities in the future.

Skills

University not only teaches you the tactical skills you will need to succeed, it can also provide the foundation for advanced thinking in a variety of academic studies, be they in the Sciences or Arts, and it will also teach you how to be an accomplished problem-solver. You will learn how to structure your thoughts, develop hypotheses, collect and analyse data to support your hypotheses, and how to engage others and communicate your findings in a way that encourages participation.

Leadership is another skill that every young adult can develop very successfully at university. Employers regard leadership as one of the most desirable skills they would like prospective employees to have demonstrated before joining an organization. Clubs, student organizations and sports teams offer great opportunities to learn these skills.

Moreover, beyond these practical skills, most students at university are living away from their families for the first time. University will teach you to be truly independent, which can be a double-edged sword – the main consequence of complete freedom is personal responsibility. You appreciate very quickly that if you forget to complete an assignment, then you only have yourself to blame. People you may want to work for, or with, in the future know that past performance is often indicative of future performance, and understanding this may very well be one of the most important life lessons that your time at university will teach you.

Financial outcomes

Research has shown that if you graduate from a top university, you will substantially increase your worth in the workplace. CNN Money reported in September 2012, 'Depending on where you go to college, you could pull in an annual salary of as low as $44,490 or as high as $122,500 in ten years after graduation.' The CNN Money website went on to state that graduates from top universities like Princeton with at least ten years' experience earn an average of $137,000. Compared to this, graduates from the lesser universities average an annual pay packet of around $45,000.

In the UK, graduates from top universities average £25,000–£29,000 after graduation from top universities like Oxford, Cambridge and the London School of Economics, with the average graduate salaries at around £19,000 or less, according to *The Complete University Guide UK*. Please note that this number for UK universities is for graduate starting salaries, and not for an eventual average salary after ten years.

The following table from *The Complete University Guide* (UK) shows just how wide the starting salary gap is between those who graduate and those who do not.

Graduate versus non-graduate salary (2012)

Subject	Graduate employment or self-employment	Non-graduate employment or self-employment
Geology	£29,182	£14,558
Chemical Engineering	£27,722	£16,000
Economics	£26,940	£16,630
General Engineering	£26,294	£19,859
Mechanical Engineering	£25,703	£16,761
Veterinary Medicine	£25,690	£18,880
Mathematics	£24,296	£16,196
Electrical and Electronic Engineering	£24,214	£15,510
Aeronautical and Manufacturing Engineering	£24,133	£16,008
Physics and Astronomy	£23,964	£16,687
Civil Engineering	£23,707	£15,774
Social Work	£23,445	£14,391
East and South Asian Studies	£22,922	£18,429
Complementary Medicine	£22,818	£14,205
Computer Science	£22,793	£15,780

Nursing	£22,626	£17,403
Politics	£22,479	£15,251
Business and Management Studies	£22,103	£15,910

2

Which Are the Top Universities?

In 2014, according to the *QS* university rankings, *US News* university guide and the *Times Higher Education* world rankings guide, the majority of the top universities are in the US, UK, Canada, Europe, Australia and Asia, in no particular order. It's also important to remember that the following league table rankings vary slightly year-on-year due to different assessment criteria by different news media companies and the changes in university characteristics. However, there are a handful of universities that regularly appear in the league tables. Please use this as a guide only.

In this book, we will concentrate on English-speaking countries and universities. Our analysis will focus on institutions in the US, UK, Canada and Australia.

Top 20 US universities by US News *ranking (2013)*

Rank	University	Location	Tuition* per year	Acceptance rate	SAT 1** 2400 scale	GPA**
1=	Harvard University (Ivy)	Cambridge, MA	$40,866	6.3%	2100–2349	3.80–4.00
1=	Princeton University (Ivy)	Princeton, NJ	$38,650	8.5%	2205–2361	3.90–4.00
3	Yale University (Ivy)	New Haven, CT	$42,300	7.7%	2190–2370	3.89–4.00
4=	Columbia University (Ivy)	New York, NY	$47,246	7.0%	2181–2340	3.85–4.00
4=	University of Chicago	Chicago, IL	$44,574	16.3%	2151–2340	3.79–4.00
6=	Massachusetts Institute of Technology	Cambridge, MA	$42,050	9.7%	2190–2349	3.85–4.00

Rank	University	Location	Tuition* per year	Acceptance rate	SAT 1** 2400 scale	GPA**
6=	Stanford University	Stanford, CA	$41,787	7.1%	2100–2340	3.80–4.00
8=	Duke University	Durham, NC	$43,623	14.0%	2190–2340	3.83–4.00
8=	University of Pennsylvania (Ivy)	Philadelphia, PA	$43,738	12.4%	2100–2340	3.80–4.00
10=	California Institute of Technology	Pasadena, CA	$39,588	12.8%	2100–2340	3.75–4.00
10=	Dartmouth College (Ivy)	Hanover, NH	$45,042	10.1%	2190–2349	3.85–4.00
12	Northwestern University	Evanston, IL	$43,779	18.0%	2070–2310	3.70–4.00
13	Johns Hopkins University	Baltimore, MD	$43,930	18.4%	2001–2250	3.78–4.00
14	Washington University of St Louis	St Louis, MO	$43,705	16.5%	2130–2319	3.75–4.00
15=	Brown University (Ivy)	Providence, RI	$43,758	8.9%	2130–2340	3.85–4.00
15=	Cornell University (Ivy)	Ithaca, NY	$43,413	18.0%	2070–2306	3.80–4.00
17=	Rice University	Houston, TX	$37,292	18.8%	2151–2340	3.80–4.00
17=	University of Notre Dame	Notre Dame, IN	$42,971	24.3%	2031–2265	3.68–4.00
17=	Vanderbilt University	Nashville, TN	$42,118	16.4%	2070–2331	3.70–4.00
20	Emory University	Atlanta, GA	$42,980	26.7%	2010–2246	3.66–4.00

* Tuition is the same for local and international students
** SAT and GPA are for the range 25th to 75th percentile

Top 15 UK universities by UK Guardian ranking (2013)

Rank	University	Location	Tuition per year – local students	Tuition per year – international students	Acceptance rate
1	University of Cambridge	Cambridge, England	£9,000	£13,000– £20,000 £33,000 (Medicine)	21.9%
2	University of Oxford	Oxford, England	£3,500– £9,000	£13,000– £20,000 £30,000 (Medicine)	18.4%
3	London School of Economics	London, England	£8,500	£15,168	13.8%
4	University of St Andrews	Fife, Scotland	£9,000	£15,460	10.0%
5	Warwick University	Coventry, England	£9,000	£9,000– £16,000	11.1%
6	University College of London	London, England	£9,000	£14,750– £19,500	11.9 %
7	Durham University	County Durham, England	£9,000	£13,300– £17,000	16.7 %
8	Lancaster University	Lancaster, England	£9,000	£14,245	–
9	University of Bath	Bath, England	£9,000	£10,750– £16,500	8.3%– 13.8% (depends on course)
10	University of Exeter	Exeter, England	£9,000	£14,500– £17,000	15.4%
11	Loughborough University	Loughborough, England	£9,000	£13,250– £16,750	14.5%
12	University of Surrey	Surrey, England	£9,000	£11,580– £14,470	12.9%

Rank	University	Location	Tuition per year – local students	Tuition per year – international students	Acceptance rate
13	Imperial College London	London, England	£9,000	£22,500– £25,000 £39,150 (medicine)	16.9%
14	University of Glasgow	Glasgow, Scotland	£6,750– £9,000	£12,000– £16,500 £30,000 (medicine)	–
15	University of Edinburgh	Edinburgh, Scotland	£9,000	£13,300– £17,500	38.6%

Top 10 English-speaking Canadian universities by QS ranking (2013)

Rank	University	Location	Tuition per year – local students	Tuition per year – international students	Provincial Canadian exams*
1	McGill University	Montreal, Canada	$2,400– $6,000	$15,000– $28,000	75%–93%
2	University of Toronto	Toronto, Canada	$5,000– $6,000	$23,000– $28,000	83.7%
3	University of British Columbia	Vancouver, Canada	$4,700	$21,000	80%–85%
4	University of Alberta	Edmonton, Canada	$5,000	$18,000	>70%
5	McMaster University	Hamilton, Canada	$5,500	$15,000– $19,000	75%–89%
6	University of Western Ontario	London, Canada	$6,833	$19,000– $27,000	80%–85%

7	Queen's University	Kingston, Canada	$5,600	$19,000–$22,000	>80%
8	University of Waterloo	Waterloo, Canada	$5,600–$7,000,	$19,000–$21,000	>80%
9	York University	Toronto, Canada	$5,000	$17,000	Mid 70%–90%
10	University of Calgary	Calgary, Canada	$3,300	$18,000	>65%

Cut-off grades for specific subjects rather than an entry requirement into a particular university

Top 10 Australian universities by Times Higher Education rankings (2013)

Rank	University	Location	Tuition per year – local students	Tuition per year – international students	Grades – ATAR*
1	University of Melbourne	Melbourne, Victoria	$6,000–$8,000	$28,000–$30,000	70–96 **
2	Australian National University	Canberra, ACT	$6,000–$8,000	$40,000–$42,000	80–98
3	University of Sydney	Sydney, New South Wales	$6,000–$8,000	$30,000–$32,000	76–99.5
4	University of Queensland	Brisbane, Queensland	$6,000–$8,000	$26,000–$28,000	70–99
5	University of New South Wales	Sydney, New South Wales	$6,000–$8,000	$32,000–$34,000	70–96
6	Monash University	Melbourne, Victoria	$8,000–$10,000	$30,000–$32,000	70+
7	University of Adelaide	Adelaide, South Australia	$6,000–$8,000	$26,000–$28,000	70–95
8	University of Western Australia	Crawley, Western Australia	$6,000–$8,000	$30,000–$32,000	70+

Rank	University	Location	Tuition per year – local students	Tuition per year – international students	Grades – ATAR*
9	Macquarie University	Sydney, New South Wales	$6,000–$8,000	$24,000–$26,000	70–99
10	Queensland University of Technology	Brisbane, Queensland	$6,000–$8,000	$22,000–$24,000	70+

* In Australia, ATARs (Australian Territory Admission Rank) are required for individual courses rather than an entry requirement for admission into a particular university. If your ATAR is 80, your score was higher than 80% of the students who took this course
** Example: University of Melbourne requires an ATAR of 70 for Agriculture, and 96 for Biomedicine

3

Finding a Course to Suit You

Choosing the right course and university

The advice for students is simple – study your passion. Choose the courses that interests you the most, do your research and check the entry requirements.

However, there are a lot of students who choose courses for career ambition, or simply because the course will lead to a higher-paying job such as finance, law or medicine. If this is the case, then make sure you research, study, prepare and know the subject very well before you apply.

And here's a really useful tip: if you choose to study medicine, be sure this is a subject you are passionate about or are at least interested in. If you are called for an interview, you are guaranteed to be interviewed by a professor or expert in the field who will test you. If you can't talk about medicine or why you want to pursue this field, you will almost certainly be rejected.

So which university is the right one for you? Is it one of the US Ivy League, Oxford or Cambridge in the UK, or an Australian university in sunny Queensland? We can't answer this question for you, but we can help you identify some criteria to help you decide.

Do I have the grades?

Am I in the ballpark for grades to the university I am applying for? For international students, it is advised you match your test scores to the equivalent in your country of study. For example, if you want to apply to Harvard, the SAT average is in the 97th percentile, which is an indication that you should have a similar percentile ranking in your respective country's educational system. For example, in the UK, a 97th percentile in the SAT is equivalent to A*AA or AAA for A-levels.

Do I meet the minimum English requirements?

Courses in all English-speaking countries are taught in English, so there is a minimum language requirement that these universities require. Usually, that will involve an International English Language Testing System

(IELTS) or Test of English as a Foreign Language (TOEFL) examination, supplementary documentation about courses completed in English, or assignments or projects completed in English. Normally, the requirement for a top university is:

Examination	Grade
IELTS	Overall score: 7.0 in four components
TOEFL (paper-based)	Overall score: 600 Test of written English score: 5.5
TOEFL (Internet-based)	Overall score: 110 Listening: 22 Reading: 24 Speaking: 24 Writing: 24

How much can I afford?

Read the section 'Which Are the Top Universities?' which offers an indicative list of tuition fees in the US, UK, Canada and Australia for local and international students. Not all information is available for all schools, so please use the available figures as a general guide, and be sure to contact the schools directly to confirm the latest tuition fees.

In addition to the tuition fees, students need to calculate the total cost based on the course studied and factor in other costs. For example, is the degree a 3- or 4-year programme, where would you be living – in New York City or London, perhaps – or does the university offer student accommodation? Here is a sample guide to the approximate cost of living per year in different countries. Please note that certain cities are more expensive than others, and the figures below indicate the average cost per year for the respective countries, just to give you a rough idea of the expenses involved:

Item	US	UK	Canada	Australia
Average Tuition	US$28,500	£9,000–£20,000	CAD$6,000–$25,000	AUD$15,000–$33,000
Living Expenses	Accom.: $8,000 Food: $5,354 Books: $800 Expenses: $1,630	Accom.: £5,000 Food: £3,000–£4,000 Books: £300 Expenses: £1,000	Living expenses including accom.: CAD$4,800–$9,600	Living expenses including accom.: AUD$5,000–$10,000

Research your university

Admissions for students in the US and Canada are usually accomplished directly with the universities themselves. These universities hold school visits, campus tours and sit-in-on lectures. They offer students a good opportunity to get a feel for the universities and their courses before making any admissions decisions. On the visit days, speak to students, alumni and tutors/professors and ask any questions you have about the university, classes, culture and so on.

Admissions in the UK are completed via a central agency called UCAS, which organizes events and allows students to talk to a course provider directly. For UCAS events, visit www.ucasevents.com. Students can also attend open days to check out the campus and talk directly to other students and faculty staff. It is a great way to ask your questions in person, and get a feel for the campus, accommodation, facilities and so on. You can find details about university open days at www.opendays.com.

In Australia, international students should apply directly to the universities themselves, unless you are studying in high school and have the status of a local student. For local students, each state has its own centralized agency to apply for tertiary education. For example, New South Wales uses UAC – the University Admissions Centre – for all standardized tests in the state, and for admissions.

Available courses

Here is a sample (see tables on the following two pages) of what individual students can study in the US, UK, Canada and Australia. Availability is variable according to individual educational institutions.

Agriculture and Veterinary Medicine	Applied and Pure Science	Architecture and Construction	Business and Management	Computer Science and IT	Creative Arts and Design
Agriculture	Astronomy	Architecture	Accounting	Computer Science	Arts
Farm Management	Biology	Built Environment	Business Studies	Computing	Art Administration
Horticulture	Biomedical Sciences	Construction	E-Commerce	IT	Craft
Plant and Crop Sciences	Chemistry	Maintenance Services	Entrepreneurship	Multimedia	Dance
Veterinary Medicine	Earth Science	Planning	Finance	Software	Non-industrial Design
	Environmental Sciences	Property Management	Human Resources Management		Fashion and Textile Design
	Food Science and Technology	Surveying	Marketing		Industrial Design
	General Sciences		Office Administration		Interior Design
	Physical Geography		Quality Management		Music
	Life Sciences		Retail		Theatre and Drama Studies
	Material Sciences		Transportation and Logistics		
	Mathematics				
	Physics				
	Sports Science				

Education and Training	Engineering	Health and Medicine	Humanities	Law	Social Studies and Media
Adult Education	Aerospace Engineering	Counselling	Archaeology	Civil Law	Anthropology
Childhood Education	Biomedical Engineering	Dentistry	Classics	Criminal Law	Economics
Coaching	Chemical and Materials	Health Studies	Cultural Studies	International Law	Film and TV
Education Learning	Engineering Civil	Health and Safety	English Studies	Public Law	Journalism
Education Management	Engineering Electrical	Medicine	General Studies	Legal Studies	Linguistics
Education Research	Engineering Electronic	Nursing	History		Media
Education Psychology	Engineering	Ophthalmology	Languages		Photography
Teacher Training	Environmental Engineering	Nutrition and Health	Literature		Politics
Specialized Teaching	Mechanical Engineering	Pharmacology	Philosophy		Social Science
	Metallurgy	Physiology	Religious Studies		Sociology
	Telecommunication	Physiotherapy			Writing
	Power and Energy Engineering	Psychology			Social Work
	Marine Engineering	Public Health			Aviation
	Structural Engineering				Hospitality

4

The International Examination Systems Explained

US examinations

SAT – Scholastic Aptitude Test

SAT is the standardized test for most college admissions in the United States. The test takes about 3 hours and 45 minutes to finish, and currently costs $50 ($81 for international students). The possible scores range from 600–2400. The test comprises three sections of 800 points each, separated into Mathematics, Critical Reading (previously Verbal) and Writing. In each section, a student can score from 200–800, and all scores are in multiples of 10. Each section also includes a twenty-five-minute 'experimental' section, which does not count towards the final grade, but rather serves to normalize questions for future SAT administrations.

Students also get an eleven-minute timed break between each section. The questions range from easy, medium to hard. Typically, easy questions are in the beginning, and harder ones are towards the end. This exam is usually taken by high-school sophomores, juniors and seniors who are applying for undergraduate admissions in the US.

Structure

Critical Reading is made up of three sections. There are two twenty-five-minute sections and one twenty-minute section that include sentence completion, and short and long reading passages. It normally tests a student's vocabulary and understanding of sentence structures, and asks students to select the best word to complete the sentence. The passages might include, for example, excerpts on literature, or pieces relating to the social or natural sciences.

Mathematics (or Quantitative) consists of three sections. There are two twenty-five-minute sections and one twenty-minute section. One twenty-five-minute section is twenty questions which are all multiple choice, and the other twenty-five-minute section has eight multiple-choice and ten grid-in questions. For the grid-in sections, the test taker is asked to write

in the answer. The last twenty-minute section is all multiple-choice with sixteen questions. Four-function, scientific and graphing calculators are permitted to be used during this exam.

Writing includes multiple-choice questions and a brief essay within an hour time limit. The essay is about 30 per cent of the total score, and the multiple choice section makes up the remaining 70 per cent.

Average score, timing and contents – college board

Section	Average score	Time (minutes)	Content
Writing	493	60	Grammar, usage and diction
Mathematics	515	70	Algebra, functions, geometry, statistics, probability and data analysis
Critical Reading	501	70	Vocabulary, critical reading and sentence completion

Grading system explained – college board

Percentile	Score, 1600 Scale* (official, 2006)	Score, 2400 Scale (official, 2006)
99.93/99.98**	1600	2400
99+ †	≥1540	≥2280
99	≥1480	≥2200
98	≥1450	≥2140
97	≥1420	≥2100
93	≥1340	≥1990
88	≥1280	≥1900
81	≥1220	≥1800
72	≥1150	≥1700
61	≥1090	≥1600
48	≥1010	≥1500
36	≥950	≥1400

24	≥870	≥1300
15	≥810	≥1200
8	≥730	≥1090
4	≥650	≥990
2	≥590	≥890

Score of 1600 implies you are in the 100th percentile.

** *The percentile for the perfect score was 99.98 on the 2400 scale and 99.93 on the 1600 scale.*

† *99+ means better than 99.5 per cent of test takers.*

For more information on SAT examinations please visit www.collegeboard.org.

The alternative examination system used in the US is the ACT Examination, which is very similar to the SAT. For more information please visit www.actstudent.org.

It is recommended that international students sit for the SAT or ACT, and include their transcripts from high school in their application. The standardized exam is a key way for US universities to rank your ability against other candidates. If English is not your first language, be sure to check the requirements for IELTS and TOEFL exams.

UK examinations

A-levels, or the General Certificate of Education Advanced Level (GCE Advanced Level), is an academic qualification offered by the educational institutions in England, Wales and Northern Ireland for students completing secondary or pre-university education. It is also offered in Scotland, but under an alternative qualification. Admission is mainly based on academic results.

A-levels are recognized by many universities and as such are used as the basis for conditional admissions offers on predicted A-level grades. The A-levels are a subject-by-subject examination which assesses a student's strengths and ability to demonstrate understanding in specific, pre-chosen subjects rather than a standardized test for all students.

A-level subjects are offered over a two-year period, within which examinations are held at the end of each year; these are administered by an official assessment body. The A-levels are completed in Year 12 and Year 13 (age 16–18), either in a secondary school or a sixth-form college for further education. AS Level and the A2 Level are taken at the end of each year respectively. Students can take a minimum of three subjects, but some students do take more than five.

Grading system – Universities and Colleges Admissions Service (UCAS)

Grade	Percentile
A*	Students who achieved an A in all A-level subjects
A	Top 10% (90th percentile)
B	Next 15% (75th–90th percentile)
C	Next 10% (65th–75th percentile)
D	Next 15% (50th–65th percentile)
E	Next 20% (30th–50th percentile)
O (Ordinary Level or Pass)	Next 20% (10th–30th percentile)
Fail	Final 10% (10th percentile)

Subjects that can be taken at A-level are determined by the five UK examination boards – AQA, OCR, Edexcel, WJEC and CCEA:

A-level subjects – UCAS

Accounting	Anthropology	Arabic	Archaeology
Art and Design	Bengali	Biology	Business Studies
Chemistry	Chinese	Citizenship	Classical Civilization
Computing	Creative Writing	Critical Thinking	Dance
Drama (and Theatre Studies)	Design and Technology	D&T: Food Technology	D&T: Product Design
D&T: Textiles	Dutch	Economics	Electronics
English Language	Environmental Studies/ Technology	Film Studies	French
General Studies	Geography	Geology	German
Government and Politics	Greek	Gujarati	Health and Social Care

Hebrew (Modern/ Biblical)	History	History of Art (and Design)	ICT
Irish	Italian	Latin	Law
Mathematics	Media Studies	Music	Music Technology
Punjabi	Persian	Philosophy	Physical Education
Physics	Polish	Portuguese	Psychology
Religious Studies	Russian	Sociology	Spanish
Sports Science	Statistics	Turkish	Urdu
Welsh			

For more information on A-levels, please visit www.britishcouncil.org.

The other examination used in the UK is the International Baccalaureate Diploma Programme (IBDP). For more information please visit www.ibo.org.

International students are not required to sit A-levels, although they can sit the IBDP exams. Students can apply to UK universities using the university entrance examination scores from their respective countries and include their transcripts for high school in their application. If English is not your first language, be sure to check the requirements for IELTS and TOEFL exams.

Canadian examinations

Entrance into a Canadian university or college varies from province to province, but basically requires the completion of a 'high-school diploma' such as the Ontario Secondary School Diploma (OSSD). This means that the student has successfully passed a provincial or federal 'literacy test' – i.e., the Ontario Secondary School Literacy Test; and successfully passed a certain number of credits – i.e., thirty credits in Ontario in a Canadian secondary school system.

In addition, some students are required to complete forty hours of community service or volunteer work to graduate.

The Ontario Secondary School Diploma is granted to high-school graduates in the province of Ontario and applied to grades 9–12. To obtain the OSSD, a student needs to complete the following credits:

Ontario Secondary School Diploma (OSSD) system

Credits	Subject
4 credits	First language (English or French)
3 credits	Mathematics, at least one grade in 11 or 12
2 credits	Science, one grade in grade 9, and one in grade 10
1 credit	Canadian History in grade 10
1 credit	Geography in grade 9
1 credit	Arts
1 credit	Health and Physical Education
1 credit	Secondary languages, e.g., Mandarin
0.5 credit	Career Studies in grade 10
0.5 credit	Civics in grade 10

In addition, also 1 credit from each of the 3 groups:

Group	Subject
Group 1	Aboriginal Language, Classical or International Language, Social Science, Humanities, Canadian and World Studies, Career Education
Group 2	Health and Physical Education, Arts, Business Studies, Cooperative Education
Group 3	Science, Technological Education, or Cooperative Education

In Canada, there is a big difference between colleges and universities. Colleges are usually more suited to individuals who seek vocational careers like roles in the catering and hospitality industries, or who wish to become electricians or a plumbers. University is for academic careers, where a university degree is a prerequisite for entrance into professional educational bodies, such as law school, business school, medical school and so on.

Admission into a Canadian university is straightforward, and it is mainly based on academic results.

International students are eligible to apply to the individual universities directly with their academic results from their country of origin after converting the grades to a Canadian equivalent grade. As Canada is an English- and French-speaking country, students will be required to pass a TOEFL or IELTS test, or a French equivalent exam (if applying to Montreal, for example).

Australian examinations

Australia uses a Federal system that is responsible for education and admissions into college and undergraduate degrees. This Federal system is divided into different states: New South Wales, Victoria, Northern Territory, Queensland, South Australia, Tasmania and Western Australia.

New South Wales, for example, uses a Higher School Certificate (HSC) system, which details a student's grades in Year 11 and 12. Students can study up to twelve units of credit. Courses are normally two units of credit, and some special courses such as Mathematics and English have 'Extension 1 and 2'. That means students taking those special courses are studying at a higher grade than the normal 2 units of credit; i.e., 3-unit or 4-unit Maths or English.

The Australian system is very similar to the UK system where students are examined through a subject-by-subject assessment and tests. Students can choose a comprehensive range of subjects including Mathematics, English, Physics, Chemistry, Biology, Economics, Business Studies, Languages, Modern or Ancient History and Music.

Although students in New South Wales will study twelve units, only ten units will be counted towards their final grade where they will be awarded an ATAR – Australian Tertiary Admission Rank. The extra two units is a 'safety net' for students. A student with an ATAR of 95 means he/she is ranked in the top 5 per cent of students in Australia. The maximum ATAR is 99.95. Other states have similar systems.

International students are not required to complete an ATAR, but are eligible to apply to the individual universities directly with their academic results from their country after converting the grades to an Australian equivalent grade. For example, a Bachelor of Commerce is around an ATAR of 95, which means that students will generally need to rank in a similar percentile in their country. As Australia is an English-speaking country, students will be required to pass a TOEFL or IELTS test.

Examples of commonly accepted international examinations

Country	Qualification
Australia	Australian Year 12: SACE, NSW/ACT UAI, TAS/WA TER, VIC TER, QLD OP, or ATAR (Australian Tertiary Admissions Rank)
Brunei	GCE Advanced Level Examination
Canada	Provincial High-School Diploma (e.g. Ontario Secondary School Diploma – OSSD)
Germany	Abitur
Hong Kong	Hong Kong Diploma of Secondary Education
India	All-India Senior Secondary Certificate (CBSE, New Delhi), Indian School Certificate (ISC), Maharashtra, Karnataka, Andra Pradesh, Tamil Nadu State Board Examination
Indonesia	Indonesia SMA3 (Graduate Certificate of Completion)
Malaysia	GCE Advanced Level Examination, Matrikulasi, STPM Examination, Unified Entrance Certificate (UEC)
Mauritius	GCE Advanced Level Examination
Norway	Vitnemal den Videregaende Skole
Singapore	GCE Advanced Level Examination
Sweden	Slutbetyg or Avgangsbetyg
People's Republic of China	Gao Kao Examination
Sri Lanka	GCE Advanced Level Examination
Thailand	Matayom 6 with Thailand Certificate of Secondary Education
UK	GCE Advanced Level Examination
Vietnam	Bang Tot Nghiep Trung Hoc Pho Thong
Worldwide	International Baccalaureate

5

When to Apply

US application timeline

NB: Admissions are different for each university – this is a general guideline

Date	Event	Explanation
Start 1–1.5 years before enrolment (Spring / Summer Entry)	Preparation and Research	Choose 4–6 universities you want to apply to. Confirm what type of degree you want to apply for – i.e. 3- or 4-year programme. Start studying for your admissions test.
1 August	Applications open	Begin your applications, as universities begin to open their applications. If you have not taken the admissions test: SAT: 6 October, 3 November, 1 December, 26 January, 4 May and 1 June (approximate dates) ACT: 27 October, 8 December, 9 February, 13 April, 8 June (approximate dates)
September	Request transcripts and references	Ask your secondary school for academic transcripts; ask your referees for 2–3 reference letters.
September	College Fair	If you can, attend the US study fair in your country of residence.
Mid-October / Early November	Deadline 1	Early-decision / early-action deadline

Date	Event	Explanation
Mid-December	Decision 1	Early-decision / early-action applicants will receive admissions and funding decisions by post or email.
January–March	Deadline 2	Regular application deadline – most are in January. NB: also apply for external funding, scholarships together with your application.
Late March – 1 April	Decision 2	Regular applicants will receive admissions and university funding decisions by post or email.
1 May	Notification	Notify universities of your decisions and pay a non-refundable deposit to hold your place.
May–July	VISA application	Start your VISA application process.
May–July	VISA application	Complete your VISA interview at the US Embassy.
August / September	Orientation	Attend new student and international student orientation day.

UK application timeline

The UK follows a standard application system for all universities:

Date	Event	Explanation
March to September	Research schools and courses	Opportunities for students to research, explore and learn about the courses and universities that are offered. It gives a chance for students to attend Open Days, conferences and Higher Education fairs, which take place between March and early October.
Mid-September	Applications open	Applications to UCAS are open, and students can make up to 5 choices.

15 October	Deadline 1	Deadline for UCAS Applications to Oxford and Cambridge Universities, and applications for medicine, dentistry or veterinary science at all universities are open.
Early November	Deadline 2	Majority of schools and colleges strongly advise students to apply before early November, which is a common deadline; this will allow time for applicants to complete other parts of the application such as reference letters and Personal Statements.
15 January	Final deadline	Final date for all UCAS applications.
End February to Early July	UCAS Extra opens	UCAS Extra is an opportunity for students who have not received any offers or who want to reject all offers from their first 5 preferences to change their minds and apply for available courses. This essentially gives you an opportunity to make a sixth and final choice. If you are eligible for UCAS Extra, UCAS will notify you of the correct procedure and all available courses via the website. During UCAS Extra, there is no further opportunity to change. Once the application is accepted, an offer will be made. You will receive either an Unconditional Firm (UF) or Conditional Firm (CF) offer for the course and university chosen. The difference between the two offers is that 'conditional' offers would convert into a 'confirmed' offer once the student achieves the expected grades at A-level and, if the candidate is an international student, clears any assessment of English skills prior to admission.
	UCAS Extra deadline 1	Deadline to choose a course under UCAS Extra
3 July	UCAS Extra closes	Last day for UCAS Extra
May–July	Decisions	Decisions for offers, acceptance and rejections

Canadian application timeline

NB: Admissions are different for each university – this is a general guideline

Date	Event	Explanation
August	Applications open	Summer session application opens (May–August) Winter session application opens (September–April)
Early January	Deadline 1	Deadline for summer session closes
Late January	Deadline 2	Deadline for winter session closes
February–April	Grade submission	Canadian high-school grades are submitted by Canadian secondary-school students.
February–May	Decision	Admissions decisions are made for most Canadian and international applicants.
March	Submit documentation	International students are required to submit required documentation.
May	VISA application	International students should apply for a VISA permit. Study permits can take up to four months to process.
June	Decision	Deadline to accept your offer
August	Orientation week	Orientation week begins
September	Course starts	Formal classes begin

Australian application timeline

NB: Admissions are different for each university – this is a general guideline

Date	Event	Explanation
December	Deadline 1	Semester 1 deadline – class starts in February
May	Deadline 2	Semester 2 deadline – class starts in July

Australia is very different to the US, UK and Canada in that the academic year starts in February and ends in December. Students traditionally apply three months prior to courses starting.

If you are a local student, or studying the IBDP in Australia or New Zealand, then you will need to apply through a central agency – for example, in New South Wales it is the University Admissions Centre (UAC). But if you are an international student, then you can apply directly to the university.

6

The Admissions Process

There are traditionally two types of admissions processes: (1) applying directly to a university; or (2) applying via a central agency.

Here we will explain both through the US admissions process (directly to university) and the UK admissions process (via a central agency).

US admissions

Most college and universities in the US use a 'holistic' approach to undergraduate admissions. They look at all aspects of a student's application when making their final decision, taking into account GPA, SAT, extra-curricular activities, recommendations, essays and interviews, and any other relevant evidence.

If you are planning to attend a US university, it is strongly advised that you begin your research and preparation for university programmes at least 1½–2 years before your start date.

Next, it is best to narrow your search to 3–5 institutions, as too many applications will generally weaken your case in the eyes of other universities or colleges. It also makes practical sense, as you'd have to ask your references to write multiple letters, and completing numerous admissions essays is very time-consuming.

Lastly, it is always good to have 'safety nets'. We advise that you apply to a few 'dream' institutions, and a couple of 'back-ups' that you will be very happy to attend, to make sure you get to experience everything that further education has to offer.

When applying to US universities, our research has shown that there are ten primary factors that will affect the decision about your admission. They are ranked in order of most to least important:

Admission Factors
College preparatory courses / advanced placement and PSAT
Academic curriculum – how rigorous is it?
Standardized test scores – SAT or ACT
Academics / GPA
Essay / Personal Statement
Recommendation letters
Extra-curricular activities
Class rank
Student interest, e.g. attending school visits
Interviews

College preparatory courses/advanced placement

College preparatory courses are ranked as the most important factor for a very good reason. Students who take college prep courses in secondary school will normally have increased classwork, achieve higher academic standards, and the GPA weight on college prep courses compared to regular courses is also higher.

A good tip to bear in mind: if you can take a course at a local college or a course at an upper level, then do so. The success in these upper-level and college-level courses is a clear indicator that you can succeed in college.

Advanced Placement (AP) courses are another important factor. If students can attain a certain average then they can take AP courses, which are very beneficial. For AP courses, make sure you don't take too many. For example, it is better to take four AP courses and do well in all of them, than to take ten and only do well in four.

PSAT

In Year 11, students generally take the PSAT (Pre-SAT) exam. The PSAT is very similar to the SAT exam, and if you do poorly in the PSAT then this is a sign that you will need a lot of preparation for the SAT. Colleges and universities do not see your PSAT scores.

However, students who do well are awarded a 'National Merit Scholarship', which is given to 8,200 students. Students who get a good SAT score, and who have a National Merit Scholarship, give a strong signal of being a consistent, solidly academic achiever and are likely to find future success at university.

Academic curriculum

The general view is that a more rigorous high-school course is an advantage, and admissions committees believe that it is a signal that the student can tackle challenging college courses.

Another useful tip is that there is nothing to lose trying a difficult course; if you struggle, then you can simply drop it.

Standardized tests/SAT and ACT

Generally, it is advised that students take the SAT or ACT twice, so if you achieve a low score then it can be improved. It is generally advised to aim for a balanced score, which means you have high scores across all test sections, and not too many high or low extremes in a section. For example, it is better to achieve a 700 in Math and a 700 in Reading, than a 900 in Math and a 500 in Reading.

A tip here for international students – especially those from China or India who tend to struggle in the Reading section – is that it's important you try to improve this section to level out your scores.

If you are confused about which test to take, here is an analysis of both exams to help you decide:

ACT	SAT
Content-based exam	Reasoning-based exam
More questions on mathematics	More questions on vocabulary
Questions are longer	Questions are more tricky
Includes a science section	Includes a vocabulary section
No penalty for wrong answers	Penalty for wrong answers – don't guess
Harder questions are randomly placed	Questions become progressively more difficult

NB: ACT and SAT exams are accepted by most universities, and are easily converted from one to the other. Before applying, you should always check that you are in the 'ballpark' for SAT or ACT grades to be admitted. Below is a breakdown of the SAT scores for each of the Reading, Math and Writing disciplines.

Table of average SAT scores needed for enrolment in top universities/colleges

	Reading		Math		Writing	
	25%	75%	25%	75%	25%	75%
Carnegie Mellon	630	730	680	780	640	740
Duke	660	750	690	780	670	770
Emory	640	740	670	760	650	750
Georgetown	640	750	650	750	-	-
Johns Hopkins	630	730	670	770	650	750
Northwestern	680	750	700	780	680	770
Rice	650	750	680	780	650	760
Stanford	670	770	690	780	680	780
University of Chicago	700	790	700	780	-	-
Vanderbilt	680	770	700	780	670	760
Wellesley	650	740	640	750	660	750
Wesleyan	635	740	660	740	650	750
Brown	660	760	650	770	670	780
Columbia	700	780	700	790	700	790
Cornell	640	740	670	780	-	-
Dartmouth	670	780	680	780	680	790
Harvard	700	800	710	790	710	800
Princeton	700	790	710	800	710	800
U Penn	660	760	690	780	680	770
Yale	700	790	700	800	710	790

Academics/GPA

A key interest among university admissions committees is the applicant's academic history or their GPA average. The GPA is generally calculated out of a 4.0 score. The GPA measures a student's academic achievement to date against other peers in their secondary school, which is usually used as an indication for future academic, career and intellectual success.

The key here is to do well and keeping doing well in Years 9, 10 and 11. Since you will most likely be applying at the end of Year 11, your Year 12 grades will not really matter. Year 11 is the most important, as it is your final result. A good Year 11 result will mean you are consistently moving in a positive direction, and even if grades are low in Years 9 and 10, a good result in Year 11 will mean you can demonstrate that you're on the right track.

GPA requirements for some of the most selective US universities

	GPA of admitted students (25th–75th percentile)	Percentage of applicants accepted
Harvard University	3.80–4.00	6.3%
Princeton University	3.90–4.00	8.5%
Yale University	3.89–4.00	7.7%
Columbia University	3.85–4.00	7.0%

Personal Statement/essay

When applying to top universities, most candidates will have great SAT scores and GPAs; the essay, then, is where it will 'make' or 'break' your application. The essay is the admission committee's way of gauging your potential and personal character.

It is recommended you do not write more than 500 words, and the ideal length is 250–500 words. From our research, admission committees receive thousands of applications, and usually spend about three minutes reading each essay, so if yours is too long, it will test their patience.

Wherever possible, remember to 'KISS' – Keep It Simple, Stupid. The essay should be short, concise, very honest, interesting, likeable, intelligent, touching or focusing on a controversial topic. It should 'stand out' from the rest. It is your opportunity to highlight who you are and your strengths, and if you have low grades or exceptional circumstances it will give you an opportunity to explain them.

Recommendation letters

Students normally ask their teachers in the 11th or 12th grades to write recommendations for courses taken, as these teachers are in the best position to comment about their academic performance. It is recommended when asking for recommendations that students prepare a 'summary' of all their achievements to help the teacher with the letter. It will refresh their memory, highlight relevant skills and help to focus on the important aspects of the application.

Extra-curricular activities

Universities like to see that candidates are student body presidents, team captains, event organizers or band leaders. There is a predominant view that universities are after 'well-rounded' students, as this adds to the class diversity. Universities love the fact that students learn from other students. At Oxford and Cambridge, they hold 'formals' weekly as a way for students to meet students from different colleges and disciplines to share ideas, learn and develop friendships.

Applicants who achieve leadership in extra-curricular activities are regarded more highly than students who just participate. These leadership positions are a sign that you can be a future leader and not just a passive bystander.

However, be careful not to overcrowd your Personal Statement with too many activities. Admissions committees can become very suspicious of students 'résumé padding', who add or exaggerate their involvement and leadership. It is advised to choose the best two or three leadership positions and activities with the most accomplishments.

Interview

If you are offered an interview by a university admissions committee, it is not optional but rather a requirement to attend. If you don't attend, it is highly detrimental to your chances of admission. Not attending is a sign that the student has a lack of interest in the institution.

In the interview, you need to show enthusiasm for the university, and say something specific about the place, the courses, the professors who teach there, or life on campus; it's also beneficial to prepare some questions for the interviewer. This is considered a sign of genuine interest.

Student interest

In admissions, students are often asked why they want to attend that particular university as opposed to others. This is often the most difficult to answer without research. So a student who does his or her research is more highly regarded than someone who merely checked the rankings.

Students who attend university visits, interviews, attend college fair days, and speak to alumni, current students or professors show they have a genuine interest in the university. So once you have done this, make sure you add it to your essay and application. Include some mention of whom you met, spoke with and what you learnt.

International students

International students who apply to US universities have additional complications to overcome. Most international students do not have a GPA or a high-school transcript. Most don't sit for the SAT or ACT, so they will need to take those in their respective countries. Most US universities do accept the International Baccalaureate (IB) or the UK A-levels.

In addition, most students might not be taught in English so they will need to fulfil additional English requirements, such as taking the TOEFL or IELTS examinations.

If the university needs to conduct an interview, it will normally be done over the phone or with an alumnus in their home country. International students are charged higher tuition fees, have less financial aid, need to complete visa applications and translate foreign documents into English. Please check with your university for specific requirements.

UK admissions, including Oxford and Cambridge

How to apply

All students applying for a full-time course at a UK university will need to apply via UCAS (Universities and Colleges Admissions Service) or visit www.ucas.com. UCAS Track will help students track subject choices, schools applied to, application details and the application progress.

Choose a course

Students are allowed five course choices and will need to pay an application fee for each choice. There is no requirement to use all five choices. The exceptions are courses such as medicine, dentistry or veterinary science and medicine, which only allow four choices. All the relevant details can be found on the UCAS website.

Academic results

It is crucial that you ensure that your exam results are absolutely accurate, as most UK universities base admissions decisions solely on academic results.

Write the exact name of the course taken at your school; for example, if you are studying Applied Mathematics, and you simply put Mathematics, there could be some confusion when trying to match your UCAS application and exam results, and that could delay or compromise any decision.

For international students applying to the UK who have completed their exams in a different country, simply submit the results from that country. Don't convert them to a UK standard, and let the university decide on what is a suitable equivalent.

Personal Statement

The Personal Statement is each applicant's chance to convince the admissions committee as to why they should be admitted. The general strategies for writing a good Personal Statement are discussed in the second part of this book, so please check the contents for further information.

Remember, you can only write one Personal Statement for all the courses that you want to apply for. So if you apply for Medicine at Cambridge, Law at Oxford and Economics at London School of Economics, it will be virtually impossible for you to demonstrate your passion for all three subjects. It is advised that you take some time to be honest with yourself, and determine what you truly want to study.

UCAS Extra is the only time that a student can submit a new Personal Statement to their final-choice university.

References

References play the same role as recommendation letters do for applications in the US admissions process. Please refer to that section for more details.

Submit application

Check – and then double- and triple-check – your application for grammar, punctuation and sentence structures.

Ask someone close to you to read it, and analyse the application from a different perspective. You might feel your application is perfect, but staring at the same details for weeks on end is not ideal. Let a third party assess its merits.

When completed, send a copy to your referee to add their reference. The fee is £12 for one choice of university, or £23 for two to five choices.

Oxford and Cambridge admissions

Oxford and Cambridge Universities have renowned reputations, comprising over 800 years of history, and alumni include Nobel prize winners, presidents and top entrepreneurs. They are consistently ranked in the top 10 educational institutions in the world and in the top 5 in the UK.

Collegiate system

Oxford and Cambridge are different from other UK universities on account of their collegiate system. Each university has over thirty colleges, each becoming the central location for a student's academic, domestic and social life at the university. At almost every college, students live and interact with both undergraduate and postgraduate students across all disciplines, nationalities and backgrounds.

Students at a college will have access to meals, social events, entertainment, sports fields, music facilities, library and so on, all in one smaller academic community, as well as enjoying the resources of the wider university.

Which particular college you eventually attend does not really matter in the long run. However, there are some small differences in terms of facilities, location and sporting grounds that might affect a student's decision. It's also worth bearing in mind that you can apply to more than one college, and receive offers from several.

Academic teaching

Students at both universities will attend lectures, classes or laboratory sessions based on the demands of their course. A major difference between Oxford and Cambridge in comparison with other universities is the highly personalized teaching methods, where world-class experts in each field will teach students in smaller classes called 'tutorials' at Oxford, and 'supervision' at Cambridge, to allow for greater debate and discussion.

Formal assessments are almost 100 per cent based on examinations at both universities.

Oxford or Cambridge?

Students are allowed to apply to either Oxford or Cambridge – but not to both. So it is important for students to be sure of their choice before applying.

The clear differences are primarily seen in the courses offered – one course might be available at one, but may not be taught at the other. Some courses may also be deemed to be 'stronger' at one or other of the institutions. Based on reputations, Cambridge has traditionally tended to be more focused on natural sciences, engineering and medicine, while Oxford is more renowned for politics, law and the arts.

Geographically, both universities are about an hour from London. However, Cambridge is a small town, while Oxford is a small city. Oxford is also slightly older than Cambridge.

Academic requirements

At both universities, academic excellence is a major factor in admissions decisions. Students are expected to achieve:

	A-levels	International Baccalaureate (IB)
Cambridge	A*AA	40–42
Oxford	A*A*A* and AAA	38–40

Application process

The deadline is 15 October (varies for international students). Cambridge asks all applicants to complete an online 'Supplementary Application Questionnaire' (SAQ), but Oxford does not.

Shortlist

Oxford asks most students to take a test as part of the application process. Students will then be shortlisted, based on their performance. For less competitive subjects – i.e., one place for three students – approximately 90 per cent are shortlisted. For more competitive courses, this may fall to about 30–35 per cent.

Cambridge focuses less on tests in the application, but more on interviews. Around four out of every five undergraduate students are interviewed after consideration of their A-levels and Uniform Mark Scheme (UMS, which is a way to standardise marking of papers across different examination boards).

Tests

BMAT (BioMedical Admissions Test) is required for courses in Medicine at Cambridge, and graduate Medicine courses at Oxford.

BMAT is also required for the Veterinary Medicine course at Cambridge, and for Biomedical Sciences at Oxford.

Sample work

Students will be required to submit a sample of their written work as part of the application.

Interviews

The interview process at both universities is very similar, and students are given either a problem to complete or a passage to discuss.

Contrary to popular belief, these interviews provide an opportunity for tutors to understand how a student reacts to new thoughts and how his/ her mind processes new information. Students are not expected to come up with the solution to a problem, but rather to explain their thought process, and this will help tutors to gain an insight into the applicants' problem-solving skills.

Practice interviewing or analysing problems with other students, tutors and people with in-depth knowledge about the subject to help you gain confidence.

Canadian and Australian admissions

For international candidates, the admissions processes for Canada and Australia are essentially through applications made directly to the university. For local candidates, you will sit your examinations at your provincial state or territory, and applications will be determined by the local central agency. The admissions criteria are primarily determined by examination grades.

7

How to Submit a Winning Application

Applying early

For the UK, under UCAS guidelines, applications received within the deadline need to be treated on an equal basis. In the US, universities sometimes admit students on a 'rolling basis', so seats may be filled up as and when worthy candidates send in their applications.

Moreover, if you are applying for a subject that is unique/niche, it is likely that all applications will be given equal treatment, but this is generally not the case for high-demand subjects such as Medicine, Engineering or Law.

If you are applying for a high-demand subject at a very popular university such as Cambridge, which has a one-in-five acceptance rate, then an early application is advised, especially for subjects such as Engineering, Medicine or Law. The reason behind this is that universities each year set a fixed number of spaces and, as applications arrive, offers can be made to meet the target required. As more and more applicants arrive for fewer places, they will increase the admissions criteria, lowering your chances of getting through.

Acing your exams

Standardized exams: SAT/ACT

- **Learn the exam**: The SAT/ACT is a standardized exam, which means every student takes the same test under the same conditions. If you learn how the test is structured, timed, and when breaks are, it will help you to identify different types of questions and target your studying.
- **Practise, practise, practise**: When studying for an exam, nothing beats doing the real exam under real exam conditions. Try to sit the test a few times – this will help you to build your stamina and concentration for a three-hour-plus exam.
- **Study consistently**: Allow yourself four to five months to study for the exam, and complete one to two hours of studying each day. This will help you to get into a routine and slowly build your stamina to concentrate for long periods of time.

- **Use study aids**: SAT/ACT preparation books, online courses and practice exams will all help you to study. Use the aids to help you identify weaknesses, learn short cuts, and complete practice questions.
- **Read**: Make sure you read short stories, articles and newspapers to prepare for the critical reading section daily. The *Economist* is a good source.
- **Learn from your mistakes**: Keep a notebook with all your mistakes. Go back, learn from your mistake and don't make the same mistake again. If you complete this properly, you will improve very quickly.
- **Read the question**: No matter how familiar you are with the exams, make sure you always read the question. Lots of students under exam conditions rush, and don't actually answer the question asked.
- **Elimination**: For multiple-choice questions, a good skill is to eliminate wrong answers first, and this will help you narrow the options down to the right solution.
- **Calculator**: Familiarize yourself with the calculator.

Subject-by-subject exams: A-levels, Canadian and Australian Provincial exams

- **Take notes**: In class, make sure you pay attention and take notes. It is important to organize your work, and this will help you to learn the subject better.
- **Interest**: Pick subjects that you are interested in, or you are good at. This will help you to study, understand and score better.
- **Prior-year study**: A-levels and the Canadian exams, for example, will take place over a two-year period – normally Years 11–12. If you study hard in Year 11, it will help you to build a strong academic foundation for Year 12. For example, in Mathematics, you will need the foundation work in Year 11 to help you tackle the more difficult work in Year 12.
- **Organize a weekly schedule**: Be strict and finish all the work you plan. Make a plan and study consistently, daily, and only have one day off a week.
- **Practise, practise, practise**: Make sure you take practice exams under exam conditions. This will help you to get a feel for the questions and build stamina for long periods of concentration.
- **Teach**: A great way to learn is to teach someone what you've learnt. If you can teach someone else, it will truly test your ability and knowledge.

Letters of reference

Who should write your reference?

It is advisable to obtain a reference from a teacher, tutor, adviser, head of department or even principal who knows you 'academically'.

If you have left school, then ask an employer, supervisor or manager who can comment on your academic potential and your performance in your profession.

Don't ask family, friends or people you have relationships with, even if they are teachers or academic professionals. Your application could be compromised as a result.

What your referee should write

For the US, Canada and Australia, each university will handle the references via their individual applications. Typically, references are now handled online. For the UK, the section on references is in your UCAS application; you will need to add the referee's name, phone number and email address. An email with a link and password will be provided, and the referees will have ample time to complete your reference letter.

How long should the reference be?

Unless specified otherwise, one A4-sized, single-spaced letter is a good general rule.

What should be included?

It is important that the referee reads your complete application to understand your course of study, places applied to, and future career goals. Ask your referee to:

- Avoid mentioning (UCAS applications) any particular university or college. It should be a general statement.
- Comment on academic performance and potential for greater success in tertiary education.
- Explain your motivation, commitment and drive for your chosen course and career path.
- Discuss past achievements, skills, passion and enthusiasm for the course.
- Discuss extra-curricular activities, awards, leadership, sports, arts or musical achievements or details.
- Explain carefully any circumstances which may have affected your academic/professional performance (mention conditions, physical illness or disability).

International students

If English is not your first language, ask the referee to mention exams, courses or education that was taught in English which can support your proficiency.

Writing a successful application essay/Personal Statement

Admissions committees received thousands of applications, and it's your job to make your application stand out. The Personal Statement, essay or letter of intent is your chance to show your passion, commitment and what you can add to the university.

- Brainstorm and decide what to write.
- Be honest and be yourself.
- Look at model essays, and take inspiration from other students. This book is a great place to start.
- Remember that the admissions committee is looking for reasons to accept you, not to reject you.

What to write

Personal Statements are a crucial part of the decision-making process when considering a student's admission, and they are read very carefully by the admissions committee. Candidates are free to write what they want, but in order to set the right context you should certainly try to:

- Explain your reasons, interest and passion for your chosen course.
- Discuss qualities, experiences and knowledge you can add to the course.
- Show that you have extra-curricular experiences and achievements.
- Explain your career goals.
- Detail any work experience – voluntary or paid – that might be relevant for your course.
- Discuss any interesting facts that make you a unique and well-rounded candidate.
- Highlight academic achievements, scholarships or awards.
- Discuss sports, music or art achievements.

NB: For US applications, there are often specific essay questions, unlike the more general approach used in the UK. Do make sure you answer the questions.

International students

If English is not your first language, detail any courses, English-as-second-language courses or foundation classes taken at school or work that may prove your proficiency.

How to write the personal statement/essay

There is a difference between listing your achievements and selling your skills to the university. For example, avoid writing, '*I was a member of the high school debating team.*' A much more effective and impactful approach is to write, '*While in the high-school debating team, I was the captain who led my team to win the Year 11 regional championships. It has taught me to be confident, develop strategies to formulate an argument and lead a team.*'

In other words, providing an overall context will help the admissions committee understand the importance and scale of your achievements.

Successful structuring

Quality trumps quantity. Some students feel it is essential to fill the Personal Statement to the brim, but it is always preferable to keep it within the word count and make it clear and concise. Admissions committees read thousands of applications each year, and would much prefer a short, clear, passionate and to-the-point essay.

A sample successful structure might include:

- **Introduction**: you should open with a clear and concise statement which clearly explains the course you are applying to and why. Strong writers may want to stand out more by using unconventional openings. Remember, first impressions are important here, so make sure your Personal Statement begins strongly.
- **Body**: the central part of the Personal Statement allows a candidate to explore in three or four paragraphs the 'reasons' why they will succeed in this course through specific examples. It is advisable here to highlight academic achievements, extra-curricular activities, work, voluntary activities, life experiences, and anything else you have done to demonstrate your passion for the course.

  Let's look at an example in which the student's chosen subject is English. With this in mind, the supporting evidence of ability, enthusiasm and passion might include: AAA in UK A-levels; starting the English Literature club at school; raising money for a new essay-writing competition; completing a short period of work experience at Collins books; writing a book at the age of sixteen.
- **Conclusion**: two to three short sentences that summarize your passion, commitment and dedication to studying the course chosen.

General tips

If you have some academic failures or low grades on your record, make sure to explain the background to these in your essay. It could be due to illness, or sporting or family commitments. It could also be that you lost focus briefly but learned your lesson and then worked hard to achieve A grades. Admission committees understand this and will appreciate your honesty.

Students often make reference to voluntary activities, books and inspirational figures who might be relevant to their course. This doesn't add value if you just write *'Albert Einstein is my hero'*, or *'I volunteered at the local Red Cross'* and *'my favourite book is* The Universe in a Nutshell *by Professor Stephen Hawking'*. You need to be specific in what you have learnt, and why this book or person has had a strong influence on your decision to study your chosen course.

Once you have finished writing your Personal Statement, check ... and check ... and check again! Make sure you read, re-read, edit and re-edit before submission. Check for spelling mistakes, clarity of sentences and grammatical mistakes. Check facts, figures and attention to detail. Have someone else read your Personal Statement – but also remember that too many opinions may not always be helpful, so only ask people who know you well and/or can add value to your work.

Succeeding at interview

Some universities will require students to attend an interview before a final decision is made. This could be standard practice for the course, or it could be a way for the university to judge your suitability, maturity and intellectual curiosity.

Interview tips

- Make sure you attend. You are unlikely to be made an offer if you don't do so.
- Be on time. You will meet with important and very busy people. Respect their time.
- Prepare, prepare and prepare before you attend. If you are being interviewed for Law, read recent articles and papers, and be on top of legal issues and recent public cases. The key is to be able to speak intelligently about the course. Schools like to see that students have a keen level of intellectual curiosity.
- Make sure you know why you are passionate about studying a particular subject, or going to a particular school. This is often the hardest question.
- Prepare an interview questions list, and write down answers. This will help you to prepare.
- Learn about the course and the university, concentrating on aspects of the course that interest you, professors, student associations and life on campus. It will help to demonstrate your enthusiasm and passion. This is also a common area where admissions committees will ask questions.

- Talk to an ex-student or current student about the interview, and what types of questions are asked. This will help you to get a feel for the interview questions.
- Re-read your application before the interview to refresh your 'pitch', and to pre-empt possible areas of enquiry from interviewers.
- Dress smartly and professionally.

Maximizing your extra-curricular activities and achievements

Extra-curricular activities on your application are a great way to reveal your key skills, such as leadership, teamwork and drive, as well as your interests.

Relevance

If you are applying for a journalism degree, and you were the editor-in-chief of your high-school newspaper, then be sure to include it.

Avoid lists

Lots of students 'list' their extra-curricular achievements, but that often adds very little value to your application. It is not about quantity, it is about quality. The key is in the relevant detail.

For example, it's best to avoid writing, '*I led a soccer team to a championship trophy…*' The better approach would be to write, '*I was the captain of my Under-eighteens soccer team who were undefeated in ten games, and won the regional championship league against twenty teams.*'

Diversity is good

If you aren't the 'best' in one thing, then being the jack-of-all-trades will always work well as an alternative. Show a number of diverse skills across all areas – sports, academics, politics, newspaper, music, the arts, and so on.

International experience

University admissions committees love students with 'international' experience. It suggests more maturity, a wider world view, and an ability to be independent. In addition, an ability to learn a foreign language or live in a foreign country is a great skill to demonstrate.

Community service and long-term dedication

Before every admissions round, soup kitchens and volunteer services around the country seem to get a flurry of keen eighteen-year-olds wanting to help. The reason, in some cases, is so that they can add a few lines in their application about volunteering. Admissions committees are experienced and can immediately see through this. Community service or volunteering is all about long-term dedication. If you have volunteered for over a year, it shows commitment and true community spirit, compared to visiting once for a few hours.

Participation versus achievement

Many students think it is a good idea to join every club, society and sports team in school to strengthen their application. This does not work either. Admissions committees look for 'achievement' in your extra-curricular activities. So whatever you decide to participate in, ensure that you make an impact, and not just for the sake of adding another line to your Personal Statement.

Part II

Successful Personal Statements

Introduction

Part II is a collection of real-life Personal Statements from students accepted at Cambridge University across a wide range of educational disciplines, together with an analysis of each Personal Statement. This behind-the-scenes look will help prospective students to understand better what admissions committees look for in candidates.

Though we focus more on departments with the highest intake (both at Cambridge University and nationally), our goal has been to select Personal Statements that are relevant to other departments as well.

Our advice is to read the Personal Statements presented in the book critically, using the analyses, too, to understand why the stories our successful candidates chose to present were key to their ambitions. Then use your own personal and professional history to come up with a list of definitive stories from your own life. The best Personal Statements are able to showcase a multi-dimensional student who will actively contribute to the culture at university, while applying him/herself diligently to the curriculum. A student is greater than the sum of A-levels, interviews and awards, and your Personal Statement is one of the strongest tools you have to paint a cohesive picture of who you truly are and where you are heading.

Good luck!

Medicine

Emily Dudgeon

The experience of being a burns patient from the age of two has shaped my life. As one of the first people in Scotland to be offered Integra skin grafting treatment and watching it used routinely years later, I appreciate the ever-changing nature of medicine. Having gained an insight into medicine, I believe it is the career for me given my interest in science and enthusiasm to make a difference to other people.

Further work experience confirmed this belief. Shadowing GPs gave me an understanding of their central role in the community. In an urban practice, I witnessed the importance of empathy and became aware of the challenges faced by diabetics, demonstrated further when I saw the subsequent microvascular damage during a day in the ophthalmic unit. After holding a patient's ventilator during a tracheostomy on the MedicInsight course, I am confident that I can deal with the unpredictable and pressurised nature of being a conscientious, dedicated doctor.

The Medsim conference introduced the practical skills involved, including simulated keyhole surgery, which was fascinating having seen laparoscopic bariatric surgery. The ethical challenges of modern medicine were highlighted by a Bioethics lecture at the Royal College of Physicians.

Volunteering at a local Special Needs Playscheme for children, I saw the challenges and rewards of this aspect of social care. Developing a rapport with a fifteen-year-old girl with severe learning difficulties, I recognised the patience required to gain the trust of vulnerable people. Following stroke patients from A&E through to long-term care, I witnessed disabilities of a different kind and so appreciate the importance of continuity of care. These experiences have intensified my motivation to be a part of the medical profession.

In Advanced Higher Biology, I plan to hone my investigative skills during my project on bacteria after recognising the importance of hygiene and infection control in light of increasingly resistant bacteria. This year, by pursuing my interest in Maths, I hope to develop my ability to solve problems using logic and look forward to utilising this in a clinical setting. By mentoring at Junior Science club, I hope to instil my scientific curiosity into younger pupils. This curiosity led me to further my knowledge of MRSA after encountering a patient suffering from this. I have also enjoyed reading the Student BMJ and found an article discussing the issue of genetic testing in relation to life insurance particularly interesting.

Elected House Captain by my peers, I am looking forward to developing my leadership and interpersonal skills as these are a vital part of working in a multidisciplinary team in a hospital. I am working towards grade 8 clarinet and play in the first hockey and lacrosse teams, all of which require teamwork and communication skills. I was proud to receive an award for service to the school community in 2008.

Balancing academic, musical and sporting commitments while ensuring academic deadlines are met has ensured I can manage my time successfully. Athletics is an important part of my life. I have competed for Scotland and have enjoyed success as National and three-time Schools Cross Country Champion,

Edinburgh Schools Champion and record holder, and English Championships 800m finalist. The commitment of training up to six times a week has reinforced my determination and tenacity. As Captain of my club and the Scottish Schools team, I have enjoyed leading by example, encouraging and cooperating with younger people, while pursuing my individual goals as a middle-distance runner.

At the age of seven, I was moved into the year above and will finish school at age seventeen. I plan to take a Gap Year which will include medically-related volunteer work and raising funds for my future education. This will better equip me to pursue what has been a lifelong ambition: to give to others what has been given to me through medicine.

Analysis

The opening paragraph blends poignancy and personal interest in the subject to create an effect of a genuine respect for and love of medicine. Very early on, Emily delves into her relevant work experience, indicating that actually working in an environment centred around medicine was a crucial aspect of her interest in her chosen degree. The first half of the second paragraph is full of specifics that demonstrate her immersion in her work placement, while also telling us things she learned, such as the importance of empathy or the pressurised unpredictability of the profession.

Her volunteering experiences and mentoring at a Junior Science Club are encouraging, but elsewhere she is a little vague – how would she go about 'pursuing [her] interest in Maths'? Still, her extra-curricular references are very impressive, and having been elected House Captain shows that people trust her, an essential element for a successful medic. Overall, Emily's immersion in her subject through practical experience and her general confidence convey a sense of competence.

Ryan Breslin

I have many reasons for wanting to be a doctor. Intellectually, I have a deep scientific interest and a strong academic record. Through my work experience and volunteering with the Red Cross I know what it's like to care for someone who is injured or ill. I love working with people and I enjoy science-based problem-solving. I've chosen medicine because I want to combine working with people in a way that makes a difference with science and something that offers a challenge.

I've tried to gain a broad experience of medicine so I could make an informed career choice. This has included community, hospital and primary care settings. I've seen the great variation a career in medicine offers through work experience in the ICU, HDU and theatres in the RVH in Belfast, as well as time in a local nursing home and a GP surgery. During my hospital experience I saw the more laborious tasks like paperwork, but I also saw how the successful treatment of a patient could be rewarding, and the procedures I saw such as intubations, cannulations and surgery all fascinated me.

In general practice, I was attracted to the long-term doctor–patient relationships I witnessed, particularly during house calls, as well as the variation in presenting illnesses. Whilst there, I learned a lot about diabetes, which I produced a project on and presented to the doctors. The parts I enjoyed most were the opportunities I got to get hands-on experience in helping the medical staff. I felt that surgery might not be for me as it seemed too much like a production line with too little doctor–patient interaction, whereas in the nursing home I loved interacting with the residents. I thoroughly enjoyed my work experience and I think that my perception of a career in medicine is now more realistic.

I recently enjoyed a visit to Cambridge where I shadowed a medical student and had the opportunity to attend lectures and see what it was like to study medicine. I saw how much work is involved compared to other courses, but the lectures inspired me and the university experience was fantastic.

As Head Prefect in school I have responsibility for organising prefect rotas as well as events and schemes such as the Formal and the Year 8 Mentors. I've particularly enjoyed the mentoring and group work with Year 8 students. I've had to master public speaking and representing others, improving my communication skills while learning how to be more approachable. It's given me confidence in my ability to lead and I think it has prepared me for life as a doctor in the sense of being in a position of responsibility.

My other interests include six years playing the flute in the school band and attainment of Grade 5. I've been involved in the technical side of the school shows for six years, which involves teamwork, learning and working under pressure, and I've also completed my Duke of Edinburgh's Award.

As a first-aid volunteer in the Red Cross, I'm working towards my 200hrs Millennium Volunteer's Award. We train constantly as well as attend public duties and so far I've achieved my Standard First Aid certificate. I love this role and find it extremely rewarding as it offers both a challenge and a way of doing something worthwhile. I spent three years in a cadet scheme run by the Fire Service and attained a number of certificates including Cadet of the Year. I learned about the importance of teamwork, working with peers and using knowledge in a 'hands-on' way whilst under pressure.

I work part-time in a petrol station, directly with the public, and I'm often in a position of responsibility when working with money. I like to use the Internet for communicating with friends and for reading; I regularly view articles about the latest medical news and research on the BBC News website's health page.

Overall, I feel that I'd massively enjoy studying medicine and being a doctor, and from my work and voluntary experience I know I would get a lot out of it.

Analysis

Ryan uses simple, colloquial language with basic sentence structures – as a result, he gives a frank and genuine impression. On the other hand, this can come across as unenthusiastic. For instance, the closing sentence is weak due to the simple language used, showing a lack of drive and determination. A balance should be drawn between avoiding too much flowery language and appearing too unmotivated.

Ryan effectively links the skills he has gained from extra-curricular activities to the skills needed for medicine. He shows that he understands a lot about the applied and practical uses of medicine, but lacks in showing his skills and potential to learn – an important assessment criteria. Although he draws on a lot of practical experience, he uses them to prove the same point – mainly that he is a responsible person. It would be more useful to include something more interesting for the reader. For instance, some theoretical references to readings on this subject and his interpretations of them would be a good idea to demonstrate an ability to absorb new material and a potential to learn.

Anonymous

People, science, challenges and teamwork make medicine the ideal career for me.

Work experiences in a hospital, a care home, a clinical trials centre and a GP surgery for the homeless confirmed for me that a career in medicine involves two of my greatest passions: people and science. I am fascinated by how different people view situations and come to individual conclusions. While debating and teaching, I enjoy expressing ideas in ways that shape my listeners' perceptions. I find connecting with different kinds of people, such as the old, young, disabled and those under the influence of drugs, particularly rewarding. My interest in people's problems leads me to look up diseases and fuels my passion for medical ethics. I organised and led a church discussion group on embryonic stem cell research. I have attended several courses; the most memorable of which was on ethics and made me question the concept of natural. AS Biology was fascinating; I felt privileged to receive such exciting information. This inspired my desire to explore and contribute to science. Wanting to understand further the application of scientific research, I spent three days with the Children's Cancer Study Group. I now understand something of how clinical trials work and the funding and communication issues involved. With my tendency to approach ideas in different ways and my interest in medical science, research may attract me during my medical career.

I am drawn to challenges. Academic successes include my school scholarships and being the first student at my school to earn gold in the senior UK Maths Challenge. I taught a group of mixed-ability Year 5 girls recorder and completed my Silver Duke of Edinburgh's Award. I find satisfaction in undertaking experiences that are out of my 'comfort zone'. I spent a memorable and highly enjoyable week working at a holiday home for the disabled. This sparked an interest in the complex relationship between the disabled and the public and reinforced my passion for caring. I work best when under pressure and, due to my many commitments, often find myself facing a time-management challenge. For example, during the first term of Year 12, I played the title role in Aladdin, participated in a national debating competition, took grade 8 flute and played the piccolo for the top Leicestershire youth wind band. This was in addition to my studies, school music, teaching, church and voluntary work commitments. I had success in all of these, and then achieved full marks in three of my five AS examinations in January. I would find huge satisfaction in the challenges of medicine.

Although happy to work on my own, I have a great passion for team-working. As I sat with my piccolo in the main square of Perugia during a concert with my wind band, I realised that my love of playing music stems from the pleasure of being part of a multidisciplinary team; everyone fulfilling their own role while acutely aware of those around them. I have enjoyed positions of leadership as a house captain, chair of junior debating and producer of the school pantomime. Whatever position I hold within a team, I work hard to be reliable and honest as I believe trust is central to all good teams. While watching surgery, I observed that type of teamwork. Medicine will provide me with the team situation I relish.

I am looking forward to playing principal flute for my orchestra at the Edinburgh Festival; performing as the leading lady in Salad Days; *and organising both junior debating and school house events. I eagerly await opportunities to explore science and face new challenges.*

In realising what I want from life and what a medical vocation offers, I have arrived at the very certain conclusion that medicine is the career for me.

Analysis

This medical applicant's vivid expression of their passion for helping people combined with a core interest in science makes her a strong candidate, particularly since the applicant exemplifies their personable character throughout the application. The applicant's fantastic first paragraph displays vast experience in different fields of medicine (common in medical applications) with the applicant's personal interest in medical ethics, highlighting the applicant's proactive and determined approach to medicine through their decision to organize a church debate on stem cell research. However, the applicant displays an imbalance between subject-related and extra-curricular activities – the essay quickly loses focus on medicine and unnecessarily discusses other achievements at greater length than those of a medical nature. Likewise, the applicant's work with disabled people is desirable and highly relevant, yet under-discussed. While impressive, their discussion of awards and transferrable skills should be more concise. That said, the applicant's emphatic demonstration of their ability to balance a heavy workload and perform under pressure is a key asset for top candidates.

Xue-En Chuang

No, the four doctors in the Singapore General Hospital decided that drawing blood from a patient for a few tests was not worth a needle-stick injury. As an intern, I witnessed their decision, made after they tried to hold down the patient who was struggling from getting pricked repeatedly. This reality has not discouraged me from pursuing medicine as a life-long calling.

My calling to medicine stems from mission trips to two developing countries, Timor Leste and Thailand. There, I witnessed suffering that arose primarily from the lack of healthcare. For a callow teenager I was then, with no worries about daily necessities, these shocking experiences evoked personal reflections – people should and could be helped via the provision of basic healthcare. That sparked my desire to want to be a doctor to help alleviate people's sufferings.

After I completed my A-levels, I was still strongly inclined towards a medical career. However, I had to be sure that my head and heart were aligned for this lifelong commitment. In what is considered as an atypical decision in Singapore, where most would want to complete their university studies in the shortest time, I chose to spend a year observing real-world medicine. A true eye-opener was my 4-month stint as an administrative assistant at the Office of Clinical Governance of Tan Tock Seng Hospital where weighty issues of patient safety were discussed. I had a bird's-eye view of some unpleasant incidents, like the accidental ramming of people by food trolleys that ran amok and patients desaturating without regular suctioning. Though I could sympathize both with the one who suffered an unnecessary injury, and the medical staff whose job could be so taxing, I questioned the how's and why's of such events.

Thereafter, I thought it would be important for me to see medicine practised in the trenches. That opportunity came when I was accepted as an intern with the Department of Medical Oncology at the National Cancer Centre in September 2009 for three months. Observing the ward rounds, daily clinic work, and gruesome thirty-six-hour night calls of the housemen has been a reality check for me regarding the medical profession; I witnessed sleep-deprived, overworked physicians overwhelmed with uncomfortable, grouchy and terribly sick patients. This experience has not deterred me; instead, it has educated me about the real challenges that a doctor faces.

In this internship, I participated in two research projects. The first involved the modelling of survival in patients with kidney cancer relating to hyponatremia; I learnt the importance of data and statistical modelling that underpins clinical research which is responsible for medical advancement. The results have been submitted as an abstract to the American Society of Clinical Oncology (ASCO) Genitourinary Cancers Symposium 2010. The second project was to collate and analyse data based on a questionnaire which asked how common mentoring really is in medicine. Some preliminary results of this study are sobering. As one who strongly believes in teaching and mentoring, having tutored voluntarily for underprivileged youths at a Salvation Army Children's Home, the results can only be an opportunity for me to try to make a difference to mentoring in the medical field.

I wish to study medicine in the United Kingdom, where many institutions are renowned for established academic traditions steeped in dynamic teaching and profound research. Thus, an overseas medical education for me will be an exchange of views and perspectives with dedicated teachers, practitioners and peers, and I am sure it will also be a course for me to prepare for life in the medical community.

Analysis

Xue-En clearly offers a well-grounded application through a vast array of experience in Singapore and around Asia, demonstrating passion and dedication to the subject and showing the application has been carefully considered. Her substantial practical experience is impressive but not uncommon, and the candidate develops this effectively by elaborating on the challenges and practical realities faced by doctors, showing she is well aware of the course requirements. Equally, her research projects are highly impressive.

Throughout the application, the candidate also shows a compassion and personable approach to doctor–patient relationships, which is fundamental to medicine. At times, she verges on unnecessary hyperbole, such as describing medicine as her 'life-calling' or stating that 'I had to be sure that my head and heart were aligned for this life-long commitment' – such passion ought to be implicit. The candidate's discussion of various aspects is nicely balanced. Her summary of reasons for studying in the UK is also simultaneously concise and persuasive, which is excellent.

Liu Hao Wu

Darwin hypothesised about the origin of life, Watson and Crick revealed its structure, but it is medicine which saves lives. My fondness for science and my respect for doctors and their work have played a key role in my determination to study medicine. Not only does it allow me to pursue my enthusiasm for science but knowing that my career will benefit society as a whole will give me great satisfaction.

I have a particular interest in Biology and was awarded the Biology Prize at GCSE in recognition of my achievements. My fascination with Genetics has led me to enrol on an Open University Course. By scouring the internet and reading through scientific journals such as Nature, *I have been learning about topics such as 'Junk DNA'. My desire to study medicine was further reinforced after attending a Nottingham MedLink conference which gave me a taste of what was to come.*

I believe one of nature's greatest wonders is the human body and its sheer complexity, in particular the immune system and the process of extravasation. As a result, I participated in the Nuffield Bursary Scheme at Manchester University where I investigated the mechanisms for expelling whipworms. For me, the excitement of medicine is that it is a dynamic subject that is constantly evolving because of research and development. During the project, I learnt how antibodies can be used in IHC. The work that I carried out will be cited in the joint paper my supervisor and I have produced and I have submitted this project for the BA Crest Gold Award. The experience has been an invaluable insight into the world of science, and broadened my understanding of immunology.

In 2005, I underwent work shadowing in a hospital in China which made me realise that a career as a doctor may be physically and mentally taxing but, at the same time, immensely rewarding. I witnessed an operation using a CT scan and was given a lecture on oncology treatment. These experiences not only allowed me to appreciate the challenges a doctor may face at work but more importantly the role that communication and a positive attitude has on patient care.

Of course, the practice of medicine involves much more than just being a committed scientist; good communication skills are vital. For the last year, I have been a weekly volunteer at a local care home which has contributed to my Millennium Volunteers Award. I accompany the elderly and also host highly popular Bingo sessions but I was disheartened to learn that some of them are excluded because they have dementia. Whilst communicating with them was difficult at first, I did not give up and eventually I learnt how to make them feel involved. In the end, it was very rewarding as I believe my actions improved their quality of life and allowed them to feel more accepted.

My leadership skills were further developed as the Operations Director in our award-winning Young Enterprise Company and my idea of designing 3D graphics was key to the company's success in the regional final. I was also the leader of a Paperclip Physics team that came third in the regional final. These activities allowed me to improve my teamwork skills and problem-solving capabilities which is hugely important when working in a hospital.

The importance of physical and mental exercise should never be underestimated, whether it be playing football in the HXCS team or simply having a game of badminton with friends. Chess has always been a hobby of mine and I have even competed in the UK School Chess Tournament. Outside school, I have completed the Duke of Edinburgh's Bronze Award which motivated me to continue with the DofE Gold Award. These have developed both my logic and analytical skills, which will also be useful in the future.

Studying medicine will be difficult, but with my enthusiasm and determination I am ready for the future challenges. Being a doctor is my dream and I firmly believe my personal qualities and desire to help people will ensure I will make a success of it.

Analysis

Liu Hao shows an eagerness to learn by including good examples of when he took the initiative to find out more about his subject. He shows good knowledge about Medicine, referring to specific areas within the subject – such as the immune system – to demonstrate his knowledge. This Personal Statement has an excellent focus on the skills the student has gained from his past experiences, directly tailored to those skills needed for Medicine or working in a hospital.

However, he makes some statements that are too demonstrative, for instance using 'of course' and 'should never', which may not necessarily present him as positively as he might like; it would be more appropriate to propose these statements in relation to his personal beliefs.

Another critique is that this Personal Statement does not convey a lot of originality and therefore does not really stand out. Whilst the opening sentence is quite interesting, the ending is rather standard and not very memorable.

Dhaneesha Senaratne

Medicine appeals to me because it combines the rigour of scientific investigation with the social aspects of caring for patients. While I find the science of the human body fascinating, I am particularly excited by the practical application of such knowledge in tackling real problems and by the impact that medicine can have on the lives of patients, their families, and even whole communities.

I appreciate that a medical career is not something to be entered into lightly so I have taken time to investigate. During the last Easter holidays, I spent two weeks at my local DGH shadowing doctors from many specialities, including rheumatology, dermatology and pathology. In the latter, I observed a post-mortem examination, a procedure that was particularly exciting to me as it was my first opportunity to directly observe human anatomy. Engaging in a hydrotherapy session was also fascinating – it allowed me to experience a different form of treatment first-hand! Shadowing a GP allowed me to appreciate the difference a doctor can make in the community, especially through home visits.

However, my holiday work as a volunteer for eighteen months at Linson Court Nursing Home for the elderly was the most rewarding. I enjoyed active participation in the care work tasks and also general conversation with patients and care workers. This summer I had the opportunity to visit a Sri Lankan hospital which raised interesting contrasts between 'developed' and 'developing' health services; particularly the idea that patients keep their own documents, with money saved on administration spent on treatment and patients free to choose which doctor to approach. I have worked at a GP's surgery filing documents, which helped me appreciate the importance of patient confidentiality, and volunteered for my school's social services programme, regularly spending time helping an elderly lady at her home.

Three-day medical courses (Medlink & MedSim) have provided the opportunity to develop my enthusiasm for medicine; a joint submission to the 2005 Medlink Pathology Project on 'The Use of Bone Marrow-Derived Circulating Progenitor Cells in the Management of Acute Myocardial Infarction' was awarded a distinction. I submitted an essay entitled 'Is MRSA a Super-Bug to Be Feared?' to the 2006 school medical prize and an 8,000-word dissertation entitled 'A Guide to Mosquito-Borne Infections' to the 2006 school science prize. A poster on Nut Allergy was awarded third place in the school medical poster competition in 2005.

Medicine, at university and as a career, is physically and mentally demanding; but I believe I can cope with and enjoy such a lifestyle. I am an academic scholar at school but I also keep myself involved in activities such as sports, music and societies. My love of cricket encouraged me to qualify as an ECB Level 1 Cricket Coach so that I could inspire others in the strong disciplines of sportsmanship and teamwork that are central to cricket. I play football and hockey at school and club level.

I relish the prospect of an intellectual challenge, whether it is problem-solving in the British Maths Olympiad or in games such as chess and bridge. I am captain of chess at school and have represented my home county Yorkshire since the age of seven, and I am part of the school bridge champion pair. I enjoy taking part in music; I am working towards grade 8 on the clarinet and grade 7 on the piano, and play in various school bands.

As House Captain of Games, my duties involve management of the sports options of all seventy boys and the organisation of all House sporting activities. As secretary of the Scientific Society, I am responsible for inviting speakers and advertising lectures, and I am also on the Medical Society committee. These responsibilities will provide me with the administrative skills needed when practising medicine.

I feel I lead a dynamic lifestyle and that I will thrive off the challenges that a medical career will provide.

Analysis

Dhaneesha shows good understanding of the practical uses of Medicine. He includes sufficient evidence of practical experience, but could explain in more depth how it has developed him as a person; at the very least, he should be prepared to talk about his experiences in the interview. Examples such as Medlink and Medsim are commonly included in Medicine applications because many candidates will have experienced the same; this candidate stands out more effectively through his essay competitions, which show a thoughtfulness and ability to analyse his subject. He points out particular tasks and specific topics that he has learned from his work experience, which works better than making generic references because it demonstrates that he has knowledge of his topic.

Dhaneesha repeatedly shows an awareness of the challenges of Medicine, and readiness to take on such new challenges. Overall, this is a well-structured Personal Statement with a coherent writing style. The ending, however, is a bit abrupt; another sentence to finish off the Personal Statement would be much more effective.

Kathryn Castledine-Wolfe

Last month I had the opportunity to observe and assist in the delivery of a baby. It stands out as one of the most exciting, exhilarating and moving experiences in my time as a hospital volunteer. I have had the privilege of serving patients in many different areas such as endoscopy, day surgery, long-term care and maternity. Each area has offered difficult challenges as well as joyful events and recoveries. I have gained an appreciation for the work of medical staff and have an understanding of the importance of clear communication, constant support and superior patient care. My respect for doctors and my desire to enter the medical profession have been fuelled by the time I have spent volunteering. The time that I have spent speaking with doctors, asking questions, discussing their specialties and the route they took to get there has further confirmed my aspiration to become a medical doctor, an aspiration which was ignited in my early teens and inspired by my school work experience at Victoria Hospital, Cape Town.

My friends describe me as committed, disciplined, focused, hardworking, adventurous and caring. I have developed strong communication skills through my experience in the corporate world and through the leadership roles I have been offered.

I enjoy being active in the community through my volunteer work, church and sporting activities: I play on a USTA women's tennis team and we are currently top of our league; I cycle regularly and just completed a weekend cycling trip to Washington DC, covering more than 100 miles; I have also been known to play team sports such as dodgeball and softball. Throughout my school career, I enjoyed playing 1st-team tennis, netball and swimming, as well as participating on the athletics team.

I have held many responsibilities within my church, such as leading the hospitality team, where I oversaw the catering requirements for church services as well as monthly meals for over 120 people. I recently undertook the responsibility for the feeding of over 500 cast and crew members at a Christmas Production during the many performances over two weekends. I have been active organizing women's events and looking after infants in the crèche. I also lead a weekly women's Bible study. Through these roles and leadership positions, I have not only learnt how to delegate, motivate and manage but I have learnt how to communicate and serve well.

At the age of twenty-five, I realize that I am classed as a mature student. I also realize that I will graduate when I am in my early thirties; however, I believe that there is great benefit in having studied at the prestigious London School of Economics, having worked hard in a commercial environment, having lived independently in an international setting and having had the experience of dealing with stress and personal challenge as well as meeting people from many different walks of life and many socio-economic classes.

These experiences have afforded me the opportunity to discover my strengths and desires. They have helped shape my dreams and create the determination and drive that I feel are essential in embarking on a medical degree. I believe that my character and the skills that I have developed will help me become an outstanding medical doctor.

Analysis

Kathryn's opening sentence is wonderfully arresting: it relates a very unusual experience, and describes what effect it had on her, adding a warmly personal feel to the Statement. At the same time, she mentions that she was volunteering – a valuable asset for an applicant – and that it was volunteering that drove her desire to pursue her chosen degree subject. Her enthusiasm for medicine does come across through specifics (endoscopy, maternity, etc.), although detailing her responsibilities would have been welcome.

Her next paragraph seems a little wasteful: admissions tutors have little interest in what your friends think of you. Furthermore, she mentions her 'experience in the corporate world', but doesn't elaborate, and doesn't refer to her 'leadership roles' until much later. Despite her extra-curricular activities being numerous (and fairly impressive), and her establishment of a strong academic pedigree (LSE), she spends a little too long dwelling on non-medicinal activities. She comes across as enthusiastic and talented, but could stake a stronger claim academically.

Creative Arts and Languages

Clarissa Parenti (Modern Medieval Languages)

Federico Fellini believed that 'A different language is a different vision of life'. I know this is true, and I want to have as wide and as comprehensive a vision as possible. I already speak Spanish, French, English and Italian at fluent levels and have been learning Mandarin for two years in the hope of soon visiting China. Since my parents are both entrepreneurs, I have been inspired by their tenacity and determination to succeed in two very competitive fields. I like to think that I have inherited their work ethic in my studies and their ambition in my quest for excellence in everything I do.

I thoroughly enjoy academic work and making cross-literary comparisons in different languages. I was one of the top ten students in the world in English Literature IGCSE conducted by the Edexcel examination board. I am writing my Extended Essay in French, comparing two novels by Eric-Emmanuel Schmitt on the theme of surrogate parents.

Since the age of twelve, I have spent many summers on courses in different cities in Switzerland, France and Spain. However, I learnt much more than grammar; indeed, it was the immersion in the target culture and the interaction with my host families and fellow students which were most memorable to me. These summers spent on my own in another country helped me develop self-confidence, independence and perseverance, qualities which I have needed in the IB and will need at University. Perhaps the reason why I study and enjoy so many languages is best summarized in the words of one of the few politicians I admire: 'When you talk to a man in a language he understands, that goes to his head. When you talk to him in his language, that goes to his heart.'

Although I only discovered Business as an academic subject at IB level, I have already been involved in organising fund-raisers for charity as well as coordinating public relations for a photography exhibition in Dubai, Paris, New York and the museum Ludovisi in Rome. This summer I also plan to work in a hotel in Mexico City in their merchandise department. A school assignment on marketing – the presentation on Ferrero Rocher's promotion campaign – persuaded me to write my business coursework on a PR and Events Management company in Rome. It is the communicative and interpersonal aspect of business that fuelled my interest in writing articles for publications such as Next Family (March–June 2009) and that motivated me to attend a summer course (July 2009) at Columbia University School of Journalism. The intensive writing workshops also involved translating parts of novels and poems in four different languages. I was known as Polyglot Parenti!

In school, I have always been involved in various activities. I am on the ZOA (Zambian Orphans Appeal) Committee, which sponsors an orphanage in Serenje where I also plan to teach the Zambian children this summer with my TEFL certificate (June 2009), as well as the 'Soccorso Clown' Committee, which funds the visit of clowns to children's hospitals. I have written articles for the latter and have developed projects for Italian TV advertising after witnessing the impact the clowns had on the children's mood. Aside from my passion for languages, I enjoy activities such as dancing (modern and classical) and Choir, where I also participated in multi-lingual concerts! I have a passion for poetry or word music, and presented my own three-page poem, written in the style of Pablo Neruda, as my Oral Presentation for IB English.

Yes, I have many interests, much curiosity and an insatiable hunger for knowledge. The university courses I have targeted are only the first step towards my ambitions. After my degree, I plan to take an MBA to widen my prospects and define my true self. I see that studying in England after my IB diploma is a natural choice for me and I look forward to the challenge of learning and exploring communication.

Analysis

This Personal Statement has an honest and personal touch to it. The student writes about her parents, uses some colloquial language and adds a bit of humour at the end of the fourth paragraph, which enables her personality to come through, livens up her Personal Statement and makes it more believable. The student uses two quotes in her Personal Statement: the opening quote is interesting and is likely to grab the readers' attention; and the second quote effectively summarizes her passion for languages. The student analyses her experiences well, which demonstrates that she is capable of understanding the new things she learns. She shows that she is a well-rounded person with wide interests outside of academics, and manages to relate those interests to her passion for languages. She also includes her post-degree plans to solidify her motivations for studying this subject. At times, however, her Personal Statement's flow is a bit jumpy, listing one thing after another without a natural connection; the structure of this Personal Statement could be improved to make it flow even better.

Alice Harvey-Fishenden (Anglo-Saxon, Norse and Celtic)

I believe that language and literature are pivotal to the study of History. They hold the key to understanding how people lived and thought. I want to study original literature, be it factual charters or ballads, in a foreign language, in medieval English or in another ancient language. How can we expect to understand a culture without an in-depth knowledge of its language, its way of life and its ideology?

In completing my Extended Project Qualification, 'How Successful was Emma of Normandy as an Influence on English Politics between 1002 and 1042?', I found that the consideration of what language or languages Emma of Normandy spoke interested me greatly. This is because it is possible that Emma spoke Old Norse which made her open to Scandinavian rule of England. To me, this is much more interesting than the obvious assumption that her role as a Norman in England led to the Norman Conquest. Writing a longer piece of work helped me to further my in-depth analysis of a topic. I am currently using both my EPQ, and preparation for a paper I will present to the academic discussion group at college on the role of language in History, as a stimulus for my additional reading. One book that I have particularly enjoyed, and found very complete in its coverage of the subject, is Henrietta Leyser's Medieval Women: A Social History of Women in England 450– 1500. *I enjoyed delving into the primary source material which she included at the end of the book, allowing me to look at sections of material that are hard to find elsewhere. In addition to the writing about Alfred's Law code and the* Encomium Emmae Reginae, *which I found useful for my work, Leyser includes 'Judith', an Anglo-Saxon version of the Latin heroine of the Apocrypha. I particularly like the way that Judith differs from the conventional idea of a religious medieval woman, modelled on the Virgin Mary. Her violence is inspired and accepted by God, and seen as a holy act, showing the mixing of Christian ideology and Anglo-Saxon storytelling.*

I recently attended a talk by Stephen Dean, the Principle Archaeologist for Staffordshire, on the Staffordshire Hoard, which has inspired me to look for work experience in the museums housing the hoard. I will attend a Villiers Park residential course this winter entitled 'Urban Britain – Medieval and Modern'. I have always wondered how people lived in the past and how they thought. I have a tendency to ask questions and dig for deeper answers than the most obvious response, which often does not satisfy me. I enjoy the idea of stories being written down to be read by future generations. I find it intriguing, especially in a medieval context, when, despite a belief that the second coming was nigh, documents such as the Anglo-Saxon Chronicle *were made. I also have a desire to understand texts in their original form, because I know from my study of French that much detail and double meaning is lost in translation. For this reason, I have started a GCSE in Latin, the only ancient language available to me at college. I have also begun AS and A2 Critical Thinking in order to improve my essay writing by enabling me to follow an argument more effectively.*

I studied Chemistry at AS which was helpful for further developing my skill for piecing together small amounts of information to create a fuller picture, something I enjoy. I love Art and am fairly artistic, but I feel it does not have any bearing on my immediate future. I feel my study of Chemistry and Art at AS level helped to keep my outlook on studying open, rather than channelling myself too early towards essay subjects.

In addition to my academic interests, I have also progressed through the Bronze, Silver and recently Gold Duke of Edinburgh's Awards with the Explorer Scouts, which I have found invaluable for developing teamwork and trust, particularly the Gold expedition, during which the team had to be very close in order to overcome pain and the magnitude of the challenge.

Analysis

Alice's opening sentence shows that she knows not only that literature and language are integral to her course, but that they are vital to the wider field of History in general. She goes on to support this interest in literature and language by giving concrete evidence of her immersion in them: her EPQ provides solid proof that she is committed to studying pre-modern cultures, while her independent observation on Emma's language and its role provides a break from more simplistic interpretations of the Norman Conquest. Her preparation of a paper for a discussion group is notable; she is willing not only to explore her subject more deeply, but to integrate this knowledge into contributions to her college community, an inclination likely to appeal to admissions tutors. That said, the last two paragraphs are noticeably weaker. The fact that Art wouldn't have 'any bearing on [her] immediate future', while a refreshing change from shoehorning the benefits of all one's A-levels into one's Statement, seems like a waste of words, while the ending of her Statement is very abrupt: she doesn't bring it back to her love for (or capacity to excel in) the subject, which is what a good Statement should do. Still, overall, Alice's desire to immerse herself in ASNC shines through and makes her a desirable candidate.

Joy Lisney (Music)

I am fascinated by the history of music, both for its own sake and as a framework on which to build my interpretation of music. Composition has become increasingly important to me and I would welcome the grounding that a study of harmony, counterpoint and orchestration would provide. I find that composition heightens my insight as a cellist and deepens my comprehension as a director, as well as being an enriching activity in itself. I also wish to further my understanding of analysis and performance practice, thereby developing my independence of interpretation.

The research that I undertook for my ABRSM and LRSM Diplomas changed my relationship to instrumental studies. Detailed research into the pieces and their context proved to be a catalyst to widening my knowledge about other music. I believe it is vital to study music outside my instrumental experience in order to appreciate music fully and take particular interest in 20th-century Russian music. I am fascinated by the ways composers such as Shostakovich responded to the challenges of composing in Soviet Russia.

Reading Nicholas Cook's Very Short Introduction to Music *also expanded the way I think about music. I particularly identify with his comments on the roles of composer, performer and listener and how they have changed over time. Philip Ball's book* The Music Instinct *explores why music is so fundamental to society. Despite its subtitle 'How Music Works and Why We Can't Do Without It', I believe that Ball has set out to demonstrate the mystery of music and examine the difficulty of attempting to penetrate it.*

I am currently working on my Extended Project and the dissertation for my FRSM, which is a study into how Stravinsky arranged 'Suite Italienne' for cello and piano from his ballet Pulcinella. *The research has enhanced my understanding of the piece as a performer and detailed analysis has enhanced my own composition technique. Stravinsky captures the idiom of the cello perfectly but retains the values of timbre and character fundamental to* Pulcinella.

The cello is central to my musical experience. Achieving grade 8 Distinction at the age of eight, I have always aimed for a career based on performance. I was awarded the ABRSM and LRSM Diplomas with distinction at fourteen and perform regularly in recital and as a concerto soloist. Recent recitals include a concert at the Holywell Music Room and have resulted in invitations to Canada and South Africa. 2010 will include Shostakovich and Tchaikovsky concerto performances and I will be widening the range of music I perform by learning Jan Vriend's Anatomy of Passion, *working closely with the composer.*

Apart from the intellectual diversity that it offers, I look forward to seizing the extra-curricular opportunities at university. I am also a keen sportswoman and a member of the U19 England World Cup Squad for lacrosse. I take part in a variety of sports, representing Richmond in athletics, and I sing in a choir competing in the 2010 BBC Choir of the Year Finals. I enjoy working in a team in sport and chamber music and value the skill and knowledge one can gain by working with experienced players. My classical education has proved invaluable in music; the logical and analytical skills I have gained are transferable to music and I enjoy applying my knowledge of Latin to choral texts.

It is my aspiration to build a portfolio musical career encompassing performance, direction, education, music journalism and composition/arrangement. I believe that such breadth is necessary for me to sustain a rich musical life in the twenty-first century and a music degree would be my first step.

Analysis

This virtually flawless application presents a real passion for music displayed throughout the Personal Statement, combined with practical, unambiguous evidence of the candidate's success. Joy remains direct and concise, without unnecessary elaboration or straying off-topic. The application is made more impressive by her specific field of interest in twentieth-century Russian compositions, giving her expertise to elaborate on in depth at the interview stage. Her discussion of scholarly literature is excellent, showing an ability to study music academically as well as practically. The candidate also successfully connects her extra-curricular successes with skills related to her subject, thereby making sports and Latin relevant to her ability to study music.

Her final paragraph is a great summary of a long-term career plan within which the degree will fit. Overall, this application could be improved by shortening the introductory paragraph to develop further her excellent discussion of academic literature, which would solidify her choice to study an academic degree rather than a practical music course.

Nyasha Joseph-Mitchell (English Literature)

From a very young age, my statutory education has been supplemented by my willingness to read anything and everything that I am drawn to. I was profoundly moved the first time I read Jane Eyre; *even though I found the language difficult and my understanding was limited, it was a book I have treasured and read many times since. Jane's character is very much how I aspire to be – she comes through her problems heroically and makes the best of her situations. Having access into other places and different ideologies has always been something I value and yearn for, and for me, this has always been as simple as taking pleasure in literature. I see reading as an activity that is adventurous and sometimes far from comfortable; rather, something that stretches my mind and forces me to confront the issues of both contemporary and period significance. I found both* Mr Pip *and* Great Expectations *to be highly moving, even though they are set in entirely different times and places. In* Mr Pip *especially, I felt able to appreciate the narrative within the narrative and how expertly they were linked to one another.*

Writing has been a useful and enjoyable outlet for me. Over the years, I have written a number short stories and poems – one of which was highly praised in 2006 by the then Poet Laureate, Andrew Motion. Poetry is another form of literature I cherish, Keats' Ode to a Nightingale *something I consider a work of art. Although it is a lengthy piece, every single word feels necessary. Keats crafts new images in my mind each time I read him, and this for me is exactly what literature should be about. I also feel deeply affected by the works of Grace Nichols, as I feel able to relate to her culturally and feel she expresses both her past and my own in a way I envy and admire.*

Secondary school was a challenge for me; I worked hard and, as a result, was given many responsibilities. As a Catholic school, we had Mass regularly and I often read prayers and readings. For a time, I was a school prefect and a supplementary member of the newly founded school council, and greatly appreciated communicating with members of school, finding out and expressing their concerns.

I set myself high standards and work as best as I can to achieve them. I enjoy working with other people but am also comfortable and efficient at working in my own space and time, as I am organised and imaginative. My education has been disrupted by mental and physical health problems, which I have worked my hardest to learn from and motivate myself to achieve my full potential. As a result, I will end my second year with an unconventional number of subjects. I am doing currently A2 English and A2 Philosophy, subjects I find closely linked as they require me to use analytical skills and think deeply about the fundamentals of society and ideologies.

Boarding in the sixth form, I am fortunate enough to be house librarian, ensuring the books are in order, placing some on display, and eventually ordering new books. Such a responsibility excites me as it allows me more time around literature.

I sing in the school chapel choir and the smaller gospel group and am hoping to take a grade 8 drama exam soon. For me, the creativity inherent in each of these activities is linked to my love of literature. Singing requires the concentration and creativity I use in my writing, and my passion for acting, which I am developing in Theatre Studies AS, is linked in with my love of studying and interpreting texts.

Analysis

Nyasha's opening paragraph is effective for many reasons. Not only does she give an example of how texts from her subject have moved her in the past, but she expresses a desire to be like one of the characters, showing a genuine immersion in literature. She demonstrates an appreciation of the complexities and difficulties of literature, and her comparison of two different texts is useful and demonstrates a key skill for an English degree. Choosing texts that covered a wider range of literary styles and eras might have been better to show breadth of knowledge, but her enthusiasm comes across nonetheless. This enthusiasm is partly embodied in her love of, and high standard in, acting – a related, but different, facet of literature. Her accomplishments and creativity are impressive – to have one's poem praised by Andrew Motion is no mean feat – and suggest that she could be an asset to university life, producing work of her own rather than merely analysing that of others. She is candid enough to admit to mental-health issues, and her assertion that they strengthened her rather than bringing her down adds to her qualities as a candidate.

Assallah Tahir (English Literature)

Writers angle a mirror to our reality, creating a world that is almost ours and inviting us into it. What I love most about literature is that it does not simply imitate but it vitalises reality, transforming it into something distinctly new and challenging the way I perceive the world around me.

I chose to complete my Extended Project on the representation of disability and deformity in literature to explore the link between perception and appearance. Analysing Hugo's portrayal of the archetype of the Beast in The Hunchback of Notre Dame *and* The Man Who Laughs *was particularly enjoyable. I interpreted Quasimodo's position in the heart of the cathedral as a suggestion that real deformity rests in the heart of theocracy, and linked this with the overriding theme of the ostracised individual in society. Comparing Hugo's fatalism with Mark Haddon's celebration of individuality in* The Curious Incident of the Dog in the Night-Time *was especially interesting when it came to analysing the ways that the narrator helps to define the 'other' in society.*

The relationship between the exterior and the interior is a theme that fascinates me. I thoroughly enjoyed delving into this topic in my study of Shakespeare and exploring the ways that beautiful, flawed women are depicted through characters such as Chaucer's May in The Merchant's Tale *and Thackeray's Becky Sharp. I find Catherine Earnshaw an interesting character for the way that her beauty seems, paradoxically, to both empower and entrap her.*

My passion for literature also inspires me to write creatively. I finished my first novel when I turned seventeen – an enterprise that lasted over three years! Reading widely made me more aware of the importance of the study of literature in my personal development as a writer, and the value of writing in improving my ability to analyse. Exploring the way that Marquez uses a matter-of-fact narrator to add realism to his magical world has made me more thoughtful in my own experiments with tone and narration. It inspired me to set up my own creative writing and literature club, where I have the opportunity to share critical responses with my peers.

To improve my linguistic skills, I am taking a course in Latin and reading contemporary poetry in Arabic. What strikes me when reading the English translations of Arabic is the sense that there is something 'lost in translation'; something in the original language – with all its connotations and characteristics – that cannot be replicated. Another aspect of poetry that interests me is the way that sound can be charged with meaning, which is what makes Louis MacNeice, with his haunting rhymes and metaphysical images, one of my favourite twentieth-century poets.

Attending a philosophy debating club and volunteering weekly as a teaching assistant for a GCSE English class have improved my ability to formulate and express ideas clearly. It helped to develop my skills in teaching and, more significantly, opened my eyes to the importance of learning from others. I hope to take the rewarding experience of teaching and learning further by continuing my

studies at a postgraduate level and possibly pursuing a career in academia. Most of all, however, I want to study English for the incomparable sense of excitement I feel at opening a book, and it is this passion that I believe will help me to grow as a critic and a writer.

Analysis

This Personal Statement is unusually impressive through its striking language, demonstrable passion and repeated references to relevant and notable literary activities outside of Assallah's schoolwork. She writes fluently and academically, thereby displaying the skills and talent for academic-level literary analysis required for an English degree. She also strikes an excellent balance between degree-specific and extra-curricular activities, and effectively describes the transferable skills these experiences give her (notably translation and teaching). The candidate therefore does not diverge from the central purpose of the application – English literature itself – a trap many candidates fall into.

Clearly, writing her own novel displays commitment and passion, but future applicants should not feel put off since most candidates will not have done so. Her brief and direct opening and closing sentences are the appropriate length. Avoid describing anything as 'interesting' – this ought to be intrinsic, and a more complex vocabulary is preferable.

Carla Bombi Ferrer (Linguistics)

Even since childhood, the similarity of my mother-tongues – Spanish, Italian and Catalan – made me curious about their origin. Why is it that words like 'pan', 'pane' and 'pa' bear such a striking resemblance? My interest for languages dates back to when, having found out that these nouns shared a common Latin root, I became aware that language is like a living organism which can evolve into a variety of new forms.

Not only did I study Romance languages. I reached an advanced level in German (ZOP) and English (CAE), which made me acquainted with the Germanic branch of languages, and studied Latin during the four years. Being confident with their grammar, I could realize that cross-linguistic similarity goes beyond 'genetic' boundaries. For instance, Latin and German have declensions, whereas none of the Romance languages has.

The complexities of translation, and how the brain works to say the 'same' thing in another language, are also fascinating. Why is it so difficult to translate Kafka with the same powerful expression of the original text? And why I am perfectly capable of remembering if a German noun is feminine, but have to make a considerable effort to distinguish between masculine and neuter? Also, language can be an issue of political controversy. Should children be taught in Catalan? Why do some people think that Catalan and Valencian are different languages (if they aren't?).

So, speaking, writing and reading in a number of languages made me enthusiastic about the study of their structure and use. I still have many more questions yet to surface about language and, by studying linguistics, I will find explanations and gain a deeper understanding of a phenomenon I am passionate about: language.

As my questions show, Linguistics links many other disciplines such as Biology, Politics, History and Literature and, to a certain degree, unites Science and Humanities. This directly affected my subject choice at the German 'Gymnasium'. Though my focus was predominantly Humanities based, I studied Maths and Physics until class 12, leading to work experience as a support teacher of Maths and German from 2007–2010. My linguistic knowledge also enabled me to work as an interpreter for an international group of headteachers visiting Spanish schools in the framework of the Comenius Project.

Life outside studying included extra-curricular activities such as participating regularly in the development of the school magazine, writing on school current affairs and events. Another area of note was in Music. I sang in the choir 'Pequenos Cantores de Valencia', and studied piano for ten years at the conservatory of Valencia. These studies enabled me to play in several concerts and win the third prize in singing in the regional contest 'Jugend Musiziert' in 2008. My attendance in English courses (Advanced and Proficiency Level) at the British Council and in the UK from 2008–2010 has sharpened my interest for a language with a phonemic system which makes most Spaniards shiver!

In Year 10, I spent part of the Summer Term studying at a secondary school in north London. From these experiences, I gained the impression that the UK is a country characterized by high academic standards and culturally rich, an ideal place to study Linguistics, a course not offered in Spain and barely mentioned in German rankings. I feel confident that the UK is the best place for the next stage of my studies and will give me the opportunity to become fully involved in the social and academic life while studying.

Analysis

The opening – claiming a lifelong love for the subject – is a little clichéd, but is mitigated by the fact that Carla has three 'mother tongues'. She goes on to raise an interesting rhetorical question, and makes a compelling point about the evolution of language. Questions like this demonstrate Carla's enthusiasm for analysing her subject and recognising its complexities. However, bear in mind that rhetorical questions should be kept to a minimum. Carla is obviously an accomplished linguist, having worked as a translator, and hints that her subject can be useful in linking other disciplines, although it would have been helpful if she had explained this link further. It's useful to read about her musical abilities, but her paragraph on her work for the school magazine seems tokenistic. Carla's specificity as to why she wants to study in the UK works in her favour, as it shows that she has given real thought to pursuing her studies further. Carla's Statement is charming, and while her extra-curricular activities aren't as numerous as those of many other candidates, her enthusiasm for and proficiency in her subject are probably the main reason for her success.

John Black (Modern Medieval Languages)

As member states within the European Union create stronger links with each other, Britain needs to be more internationally engaged. Britain tends towards complacency with language skills, though clearly this is not entirely the fault of the British people, since English is so prominent in today's world that it is often seen as unnecessary to learn languages. I believe, however, that one cannot fully appreciate the richness of another culture without the study of language. I agree with Benjamin Whorf's view that a person's language affects the way they view the world and so the way in which they think; this means that you cannot completely understand another person, or even an entire nation, without some knowledge of their language. As a consequence of allowing understanding, language has the potential to unite nations. Because of this, I think that by advancing one's knowledge of languages, one can be more integrated with the world as a whole, rather than being limited by nationality.

Unfazed by the absence of Italian teachers at school, I studied Italian on my own for four years and successfully took it to GCSE level. Last year, I held an Italian taster session with great success to introduce people to the language. Many people feel that language study is difficult, and it can be. However, it is a difficulty which, I think, brings rewards far greater than the effort put in. I find that the intricate, almost beautiful, nature of language provides more than enough reward in itself. Therefore, I am prepared to work as hard as I possibly can to increase my proficiency with languages. It is a lifelong form of study and, since I know that I will never be satisfied with my language skills, I also know that I am capable of dedicating myself to serious study at university. The fact that, in an extremely successful academic school, I have won both the French and German prizes in the past two years for being the most accomplished linguist in the year proves this.

I often use my language skills outside of school – for example, through literature. I find that the literature of each country is unique. I am currently reading 'L'elegance du herisson by Muriel Barbery and have derived enormous benefit and enjoyment from it. I read as much foreign literature as possible, since it is something that I enjoy and is a window into the mindset of entire cultures. I am interested in both literature and the more linguistic sides of language; for example, in my 4,000-word Extended Essay I wrote about the philosophy of language.

In addition to literature and linguistics, I have been using languages whilst volunteering at Paignton Zoo for the past two years. It has boosted my confidence in my interpersonal skills, and has also helped me to improve my skills in many other areas. I have often needed to speak to visitors who have encountered problems because they are unable to speak English very well, and I also helped a French colleague during an exchange programme. The chance to use my language skills in practice was enjoyable and a challenge which I truly relished.

In the face of falling numbers of students taking language GCSEs, I decided to try and encourage language learning in my school. To make the most difference, I directed my efforts at both students and their parents. This not only meant that there was more opportunity for language learning in school, but also more encouragement at home. For eight weeks, therefore, I taught a beginners' French course to the parents of students, without help from a language teacher. I also ran a language club where students could start to learn Italian or have help with their French. This was hugely successful, with the group often consisting of up to thirty students who wished to improve their language abilities. As you can see, I am a dedicated and highly organised student, am enthusiastic, and have a natural love for language. I, therefore, think that I would be perfect for your course.

Analysis

John begins very strongly, and continues in this vein throughout the Statement. Demonstrating his analytical skills by dissecting Britain's linguistic insularity, he is clearly an intelligent student who believes keenly in the power and value of languages. He shows extraordinary initiative by having learnt Italian on his own for four years, as well as independently encouraging parents to take up French, and makes no secret of his enthusiasm for the language. John isn't just keen, though – he's clearly an accomplished, prize-winning linguist, and his desire to learn more extends into his spare time. Such melding of the academic and leisure spheres showcases John as a serious language enthusiast. Despite being stimulated by his subject, John doesn't seem insular; in several places he shows that he is good at connecting with people. This Statement is powerful largely because of John's obvious confidence, which is backed up by his initiative and his accomplishments. It helps that the opening and closing paragraphs contain an opinion of limited language-learning on a national scale, indicating that John is aware of the context of his desire to study MML.

Anna-Luise Wagner (Modern Medieval Languages)

I am fortunate in having travelled quite widely and to have come into contact with a diverse range of cultures, be it through drinking tamarind in Costa Rica, dancing Merengue in the Seychelles, eating parsnips in England, shark soup in China, or sea urchin in France. Most frequent visits have been to France, staying with the family of my exchange partner.

While collecting experiences of French family life (and local food!), I also encountered French literature for the first time in the form of a torn copy of Le Petit Prince. *Current study of French 'classics' of the nineteenth century is allowing me to compare the presentation and development of adulterous relationships in Flaubert's* Madame Bovary *and Stendhal's* Le Rouge et le Noir *for my IB Extended Essay. I am enjoying the close textual analysis, especially of the rich, insightful descriptions of character. I have followed on with the theme of adultery, class and life of women through independent reading of* Nana *by Zola and Collette's* La Vagabonde. *Naturally, my curiosity for literature is not only confined to French authors, but ranges from German classics like* Effi Briest *to Italian writers such as Tomasi di Lampedusa.*

I have frequently travelled to Italy with my family to visit friends. While in Italy this summer, attending my annual singing course near Siena, I discovered that while my French and Latin have allowed me to understand much, I responded in Spanish! My current extra-curricular Italian course should help with this. My interest and success in my study of Spanish, German, English, Latin and Greek have given me a secure academic foundation from which to approach a degree in Modern Languages with confidence and enthusiasm. I am particularly looking forward to a course which will enable me to study literature, film and the history of France and Italy in more depth.

My work experiences in the Musical Academy in Cologne, in a law firm in Germany and the town hall in Versailles introduced me to several potential careers which music and languages may offer, while developing my speaking skills and my approach to solving problems. Coming into contact with people from different cultural backgrounds is a major motivation for my future career intentions: diplomacy and international law are possible options.

In addition to my academic work, my passion for singing prompted me to start learning Italian, the language of opera. I have won several first prizes in local and regional competitions and a third prize in a national competition and have performed with numerous choirs. At Malvern College whilst singing in the school chapel choir, I have also had some fun with musical theatre – most recently I was Cosette in Les Misérables. *I enjoy performing and it encourages me to think and act independently. For my Grade 7 in drama, I chose monologues from* Romeo and Juliet *and* The Good Person of Szechwan, *and I am currently working on a monologue of* Phèdre *together with an extract from* Le Misanthrope. *With Stratford-upon-Avon nearby, I have been fortunate enough to see several Shakespeare plays.*

Although I pursue sports based on individual effort, endurance, self-discipline and concentration such as tennis, lifeguard swimming and shooting, it is important for me that my team skills are not neglected. Hence I participate in activities such as Gold Duke of Edinburgh's Award scheme and the CCF. My election as one of the College Peer Mentors provides me with the opportunity to use my communication and listening skills. I have also been invited to join the school's elite scholars' society, giving me the chance to discuss cultural topics with my peers including, recently, themes such as colonialism and Steiner education.

I am very excited by the prospect of being able to continue with and develop my academic, musical and other interests at university, and very much look forward to rising to the challenges on offer.

Analysis

Anna-Luise's application for French and Italian begins with a colourful and lively introduction, but widespread travel is an asset and not a necessity; tutors know most applicants will not have had such opportunities. The success of Anna-Luise's application lies in her ability vividly to portray her passion for languages and literature, sharpened by her light tone and occasional humour, although her grammar is sometimes poor. Emphasising novels she has enjoyed across various cultures and languages is key to her application, since the MML course focuses heavily on literature. However, Anna-Luise's discussion of languages ends far too quickly, and she discusses her interests in music, drama and sport at too great a length. She conveys her all-rounded, enthusiastic character, complemented by her strong focus on the personal skills she has gained, but this ought to be more concise and secondary to her central focus on languages. Anna-Luise has evidently tried to maximize her experience with foreign language and culture, which is central to her success.

Social Studies

Matthew Egerton (Economics)

'The ideas of economists...are more powerful than is commonly understood. Indeed, the world is ruled by little else.' This quote from Keynes began to mean something to me whilst reading the first page of Levitt's Freakonomics. *I find the application of Economics-related ideas in all walks of life, as highlighted by Levitt and Keynes, uniquely appealing. A subject whose roots affect real lives, in real situations, meaning things to real people, is a subject whose walls of application are infinitely vast and whose pool of problems are deeply important to address. This is what first attracted me to Economics and now I wish to explore deeper into this pool, to understand more.*

I have taken great interest in the stock market from an early age, having held my own shares and participated in the Student Investor Programme. I read the Financial Mail *every week as well as the online thisismoney.co.uk weekly newsletter. When reading* The Economist, *I find the statistical tables at the back the most useful part, a way to look at Britain's role within the wider global economy and away from the shadow of personal opinion and media coverage. Only then, I believe, is it possible to judge our economic situation in relative terms and to take a holistic approach to economic analysis.*

One of the areas I find particularly interesting is the Wealth Management industry – the investment banking sector in particular. I went on work experience to a Financial Adviser to gain an insight into risk-return strategies and financial planning. This enabled me to visualise how the Financial Services Industry operates from the very basic level and the many different careers that branch off from this central 'spine'. I scored higher on a test designed for Qualified Financial Advisers than some professionals had achieved; this gave me confidence that a possible career at the forefront of this industry would be both rewarding and productive in the future. I also spent time at an Accountancy firm, the focus being more on tax, cash flow and liquidity.

I also have a passion for Architecture, having spent a week at TACP Architects using their CAD software. The development of ideas and the ever-changing accepted 'system' of doing things, I feel, has similarities to the field of Economics. The creative and innovative side to the subject is continually kept fresh which I find exciting.

I have partaken in Young Enterprise twice as Managing Director. The Company reached the North Wales Final and I was awarded the 'Achiever of the Year' for Wrexham both times. I relished the challenges of organisation, leadership and responsibility posed in achieving success and learnt the importance of finance at a corporate level and the crucial role of business in our society today.

I am also currently completing my Gold Duke of Edinburgh's Award. The Open Expedition I completed in Yorkshire was an excellent way to meet new people. This has helped to improve my interpersonal skills and given me the opportunity to look more closely at the way other people use the power of reasoning to make sense and form opinions about the world around us.

Recently I went to Zambia and Botswana on a month-long expedition to teach lessons and carry out vital building work at Itala School. The expedition gave me first-hand experience of the African Economy, the economic issues and, in particular, the influence of China. I was able to collate a reverse viewpoint of our own society from a third-world perspective; this I found particularly refreshing. Reading both the Economist *and* Zambian Analysis *whilst in Zambia allowed me to compare and contrast all that I was witnessing on a wider economic level.*

I believe the rounded skills and knowledge base I have developed will suit me very well for a degree in Economics. I am keen to develop my understanding and awareness of the viewpoints and reasoning of others and, in time, form my own educated opinion on the economic issues of tomorrow.

Analysis

Matthew instantly highlights his enthusiasm by having read *Freakonomics*, although he might have chosen something a little more obscure – many candidates would have read this book. Indeed, his opening paragraph is not particularly remarkable in expounding the importance of Economics in our world. However, he soon becomes more specific, detailing his participation in the Student Investor Programme and his following of current financial affairs. His general analysis of British economics as contextualised by global trends is an interesting point, showing independent thought and an awareness of the importance of 'the bigger picture'. His surprisingly high score on a test aimed at professionals is impressive as well as being a little humorous; also worthy of note is his leadership of a Young Enterprise team, which ended up being rather successful. A two-time winner of the 'Achiever of the Year' award, it is clear that Matthew has a head for business, and an ability to take charge. His paragraph on Zambia also offers an interesting angle, and complements his earlier ideas of the importance of the global nature of economics.

Benedek Csorba (Economics)

I imagine myself in the future as someone who has a detailed perspective on international economic processes and is capable of playing an active role in controlling those as well, either as an EU representative or a firm MD. To fulfil this goal, the highest possible level of academic education is needed, which, I truly believe, is mostly accessible in the United Kingdom, due to its deeply-rooted traditions in economic education, its chief position in the global economy, and its wide-ranging international relations.

I am a senior student of ELTE Apáczai Csere János Secondary Practice School, one of the top high schools in Hungary, which has given several leading experts and intellectuals to the country. Due to my curricular and extra-curricular achievements, the exact details of which I intend to present in the following paragraphs, I have received acknowledgement from my teachers, the headmaster of my school, and even from the mayor.

In my education, I have been focusing on Mathematics, History, Philosophy and Social Studies in particular. I have decided to take specialised courses in these subjects, and exams on a higher level, because, as far as I'm concerned, they can provide me with a strong basis for my further studies in the fields of Economics and international relations. Since skills in rationally analysing complex issues and understanding their background are crucial in political and economic decision making.

I also took extra classes in Geography, not only to prepare for the prescheduled final exams but to deepen my knowledge about geopolitics. During the same year, I ended up in the finals of the National Geography Competition for Secondary Schools as well. Keeping my future plans in mind, I chose to do research, on the role of the European Union in the global economy as my competition entry. In my research, I examined the current condition of the Integration and I tried to investigate its possibilities to enhance economic efficiency. As a consequence, it has become quite clear that economic policies and regulations on a European level are something I would be gladly concerned with. Owning to this research and since I was a regular participant of lecture sessions and a yearly competition of the Hungarian National Bank until recently, I have gained experience in the fields of the European and Hungarian economy and monetary policy. In addition, I have obtained a certificate in interactive innovation techniques during a seminar organised on a national level. There I have learnt methods for putting new ideas into practice. I consider these to be highly important, because there is no lack of innovative thoughts but experts who can use the ideas in real life.

I consider leadership skills to be one of the most essential requirements in both economic policies and business. I am a member of the so-called Student Committee of our school, and I was elected the leader of the committee in the previous school year. In this position I have not only been responsible for organizing extra-curricular activities for students, but I have also been in charge of their well-being in the school, trying to solve possible teacher-student and student-student conflicts. I am going to participate in the National Student Parliament in March 2011 as a representative of not only our school but all schools in our district.

I have been learning English since my early childhood and German for 4 years. In addition, I have managed to make use of these languages in real-life situations during international exchange programs, and thanks to numerous family friends abroad. I have passed the CAE at the end of the previous semester, obtaining a grade A. These facts and my habit of reading the Economist *and other economy-related publications such as the works of Mr Joseph Stiglitz surely enable me to use English proficiently on an academic level.*

Europe has succeeded in sustaining its diversity and I have always considered it to be vital task of mine to represent Central-Eastern Europe at international student meetings while visiting foreign countries in order to understand their culture. For instance, participating in the international Comenius Program designed to bring students of Europe together, I have been to Latvia and Poland, and at the same time I have visited several others on school or family excursions. These programs have had long-lasting effects on me. I truly value the relationships with people I have met from all over Europe during these journeys.

Yet I have never forgotten to keep fit not only mentally but physically too. I have been doing sports since I was a child. I am especially proud of the facts that I won the National Championship in Karate and our league with my basketball team.

Besides sports, I love photographing. I am an editor and the chief photographer of the student magazine of our school. I have felt encouraged to gain all this experience in order to take steps to reach my future goals. The most challenging of which is to help finding ways to a more sustainable and balanced economic structure in Europe.

Analysis

Benedek is ambitious, having stretched himself beyond academic work into relevant, career-related fields. He shows passion by connecting his desire to work in European economics with travel and student-level economics and politics events. Likewise, the applicant's discussion of his leadership skills bridges his past experiences with transferable skills gained.

This Statement's overwhelming dominance of subject-specific discussion is excellent, although his introduction could be shortened. He could also shorten lengthy phrases such as 'in the field of Economics' to simply 'Economics'. His concluding paragraphs covering his hobbies and a final summary are of appropriate length.

Overall, this candidate could have sharpened his application by elaborating on specific Economics-related skills, for example by discussing what he learned or liked about Stiglitz's work. Although evidently an international candidate, spelling mistakes and poor grammar should be avoided, particularly for applicants to essay-heavy degree courses like Economics.

Jack Malde (Economics)

My interest in Economics was first stimulated during a visit to my father's childhood home in Kenya. My father recalled a thriving neighbourhood from his youth. Instead, we saw a run-down, struggling community where people were forced to beg for the bare necessities. It seemed counter-intuitive that conditions had worsened with time and the poverty I saw urged me to learn more. It unnerves me that some countries, such as the USA where my mother grew up, are so economically superior and I feel this gap must be narrowed. Indeed, I believe that Economics deals with the most important issues our world faces today and development is one area that particularly interests me.

I recently read The Bottom Billion *by Paul Collier. I found it fascinating how Collier suggested that all poor countries fall into one or more of just four traps. In particular, I was intrigued to learn about the paradoxical 'resource curse' where the discovery of a resource can actually constrict growth and was shocked to learn that aid can have a similar effect. I also found Collier's idea – that democracy can be disastrous in resource-rich countries unless specific restraints are used – very surprising and the use of the media to make government activity more transparent, I feel, is genius.*

Currently I am reading Dead Aid *by Dambisa Moyo. It is interesting that, while Collier argues aid can be effective when used wisely, Moyo strongly disregards aid, feeling it helps promote dependency and corruption. I feel that Moyo underestimates the effects that aid can have and it is hard to refute Collier's idea that aid can prove invaluable in particular circumstances such as in post-conflict situations. Both books were nice additions to the study of development at A-level, which I feel has been the most interesting part of the course.*

Other than Economics, Mathematics is also a subject I have enjoyed and excelled in, achieving gold in the Senior Mathematical Challenge. On this front, I recently read Game Theory: A Non-Technical Introduction *by Morton D. Davis. I liked how Davis applied the subject to real-life scenarios and was surprised to learn how often we play such games in everyday life.*

This year I have greatly enjoyed being a committee member of 'Polecon', my school's economics and politics society. Contacting and listening to distinguished speakers talk has been great and Vince Cable was a recent visitor. Cutting spending to tackle the deficit was discussed and I personally agreed with Dr Cable on a capital gains tax reform. I was recently appointed Jon Snow's contact and am looking forward to introducing him and hearing what he has to say.

I spent a fortnight at Barclay's Bank for work experience and a visit to the exciting trading floor was my personal highlight. The atmosphere was exhilarating but a career that involves making a positive difference in the world could prove more satisfying.

I have enjoyed going to lectures at the LSE and recently attended a talk on employment, labour markets and development. The use of capital controls to coordinate exchange rates was one of many interesting ideas.

For seven years now I have played the flute and, as well as achieving a merit at grade 7, I have relished playing challenging repertoire for the school orchestra and flute ensemble. I also like playing fives, a sport that has provided me with wins over strong adult teams, the important title of 'Secretary', first-team colours and even silverware. I would like to continue both hobbies for as long as possible. In addition, I take part in the Duke of Edinburgh's Gold Award scheme, helping children with their homework every week at Hammersmith library. The award has helped me hone my leadership and organisational skills.

At times, juggling these activities with schoolwork can be demanding but, at the same time, exciting and I personally enjoy the challenge.

Analysis

Jack's opening paragraph comprises observations about economic disparities between certain countries, and goes on to state which aspect of Economics particularly interests him. Not only does he mention three books, he discusses in relative detail what he learnt from them, and even criticises one of Dambisa Moyo's arguments, showing a capacity for critical thought. He supports his enthusiasm by discussing his involvement in his school's Economics and Politics society, and seems to have been quite involved in it, although one should avoid vague statements such as 'I was recently appointed Jon Snow's contact'.

Spending a fortnight at a prestigious bank is obviously sound work experience, while his attendance at LSE lectures further underlines his love for Economics. Jack details specifics throughout the Statement, such as 'the use of capital controls', which strengthens his application and could provide discussion points for interview. If you are to include specifics, make sure you know about them in case your interviewers choose to explore them with you!

Daniel Macmillen (Politics)

My British-Russian parentage combined with living in Latin America for the past nine years has given me personal insight into the political systems and cultural values of different societies. Through volunteer work in the impoverished Argentine provinces of Chaco and Salta, I have seen at first hand the extreme poverty caused by failures of the political system as well as the power that grassroots action can have to improve people's lives. In contrast, world politics often seems to be dominated by media spin and bureaucratic structures of governments and international organisations. I would like to study Politics, Sociology and their related subjects in order to gain a deeper understanding of these issues and their potential solutions.

I have enjoyed reading a number of writers in the field of political and social philosophy such as Marx, Foucault, Dewey and Aristotle, however two works in particular have left a major impression on my thinking. In Chomsky's Profit over People *I have reflected on the links between politics and business and the economic and political consequences that globalisation and neo-liberal policies have brought to many Third World countries. These issues are actively debated today in Argentina, a country like so many others in Latin America where military intervention and bold economic experiments have often failed to bring about social progress. Gramsci's* Prison Notebooks *introduced me to the concept of cultural and political hegemony reinforced through control of mass media. I have explored this theme further in my IB extended essay on the Argentine military dictatorship's manipulation of football for political means, as well as experiencing the media's role in politics for myself during a work placement at the Reuters office in Buenos Aires. Attending the Reach Cambridge summer programme on Journalism, Media and Politics furthered my interest in the political power of media.*

I enjoy debating political and philosophical ideas at my school's debate club, having trained with the Argentine debating team and attended the ESU Debate Academy in Britain. Networking with young social entrepreneurs from all over the world at the 2009 Global Youth Summit organised by the British Council opened my eyes to the dynamism of small, local projects. Combining this knowledge with my interest in art-based education, I co-founded LSFA (Lincoln Student Fine Arts), a student-run organisation at my school dedicated to fund-raising through artistic performances. The money raised by LSFA supports under-funded educational institutions in northern Argentina, where I have also helped to build schools for the local indigenous population.

During my summer holidays in London I volunteered for the NGOs 'Busking for Cancer' and 'Kids Company', while at school I helped organise charity football matches for earthquake relief in Haiti and Chile. Being raised in a trilingual household (Russian, English, Spanish) has made me curious to learn more languages so I have taken courses in French and Portuguese. I play first-team football for my school; I also play piano, drums and bandoneon and have taken on roles in a number of theatrical productions. I took special interest in the power of artistic expression while working on Brecht's Mother Courage and her Children *and Rose's* Twelve Angry Men *due to their strong political and social messages. I also co-wrote and co-directed a musical to raise funds for LSFA and won the School's Outstanding Junior Award of 2010. In Year 11, I was elected as a grade representative to the school's student government and am a member of the National Honour Society, a student body in charge of community service.*

Academic study, personal reading and practical experience have inspired me to further explore the intersection of politics, culture and social justice. I would be grateful for, and look forward to, the opportunity to challenge and inform my beliefs that such an engaging university course can provide.

Analysis

Daniel's strength lies in highlighting his own unusual political experience of living in Argentina, and successfully combining this with related extra-curricular work and academic study. Having a central 'theme' or particular interest in one field will make a candidate memorable, whilst legitimising his claim to be interested in politics. The candidate exemplifies a firm grounding in the academic debates surrounding his field through sophisticated reading (when you are writing your own Statement, remember that book titles should preferably be written in italics), but on occasion he loses focus on *his* application. While impressive, the applicant's Reuters internship and tri-lingual background should not be off-putting to applicants without similar experiences. Indirectly relevant assets do not ultimately determine the outcome of an application. The candidate's concluding paragraph is excellent, summarizing his interests while showing an unusual humility.

Adam Terry (Economics)

When I started studying Economics at A-level, I soon came to realise that the discipline included, explained or expanded on areas of my interest which I had never been able to link together before. My early interest in History evolved into an eagerness to understand causation. I became increasingly convinced of the ability of economic factors to explain historical events, which led to a desire to find out more about economic theory. While reading A. Marr's A History of Modern Britain, *I was most intrigued by the economic history. Events such as Margaret Thatcher's abandonment of full employment grabbed my attention far more than any political scandal because of their complex and quantifiable impact. I was gratified to realise that Economics stretches far beyond its origins in the study of prices, markets and output into social and political realms. As economists increasingly apply economic method to social issues, I read* Hard Work *by P. Toynbee to discover the enduring social effects of the Government's economic policy, such as the level of the minimum wage.*

Travelling has inspired me to learn about other countries, especially their political and economic situations. The global insight provided by the Economist *has fired this interest, especially in the development of China. I was fascinated by Will Hutton's book* The Writing on the Wall, *which presented a far starker and more rational view of the Chinese economic situation than the often sensationalist press. His description of a paradoxical situation where the Party-State muddles through to a modern capitalist economy in the absence of any genuine political or economic pluralism changed my perspective on the issue entirely.*

I particularly enjoyed reading The Economic Naturalist *by R. H. Frank; it showed me how economists have a toolkit of concepts and theories which they can readily apply to real-world situations. P. Dasgupta's* Economics: A Very Short Introduction *provided a more serious insight into the function of successful markets and market failure, while sparking my interest in global inequalities and development economics by contrasting families in America and Ethiopia. I have attended several lectures in London, including the UN Conference on Trade and Development's 2010 report launch lecture which I very much enjoyed. Having a keen interest in current affairs, I enjoy L. Halligan's 'Economics Agenda' column in the* Sunday Telegraph *and read the* Economist *every week. Doing so has illustrated to me the way that economic theory can explain domestic and global phenomena and can be used to great effect in formulating policy.*

While examining the course structures for undergraduate degrees in Economics, I was pleasantly surprised by the amount of quantitative and mathematical content. I particularly enjoy A-level Maths and, to focus my mathematical study on Economics, I have been working through the Using Mathematics in Economics *textbook by R. L. Thomas. I have enjoyed studying Chemistry, so the fusion within Economics of a rigorous and structured analytical approach to problem solving with essay writing and debate makes it the perfect subject for me.*

I love getting involved at school. Last year I was the MD of a Young Enterprise company, which developed my organisational and communication skills. I relish any opportunity for responsibility so was pleased to be appointed as prefect. I enjoy sport and have played for the school 1st XV, as well as playing squash. I aim to manage my time effectively and believe that I have a capacity for hard work; I find a heavy workload motivating and enjoy the challenge of balancing commitments at school. My busy social life is very important to me. After travelling around Jordan with a friend and participating in a month-long expedition to Venezuela, I am very excited about seeing more of the world. Having read so much about the economic situation there, I am working to fund a trip to China this summer to experience it first hand.

Analysis

Adam's highly analytical and historicized approach to his subject contrasts with other applicants' more mathematical focus. He appears bright and interested due to his focus on the modern global application of Economics, contextualized historically and politically, rather than studying the subject simply in itself. His extra-academic reading, which is broad and sophisticated, is highly impressive. However, he should be prepared to be challenged at interview for his initial bold claim that economic events dominate historical causation. Above all, the candidate's specialty in China is impressive and, being topical and contentious, provides a firm basis for further discussion in a field in which the candidate is comfortable at interview – he should remain attentive to developments in China. It is appropriate that the candidate balances his political emphasis with a clear interest and advanced understanding of Mathematics, so as to balance his abilities. His paragraph on extra-curricular activities and travel is very impressive, as it effectively shows skills and personal qualities, and connects back to his personal interest in China.

Joyce Ong Pei Wen (Economics)

Economics is the lens through which I have come to view the world. I love how we use theories, data and models to understand people's choices on a collective level, and create a framework for managing our society. This is why I would like to study Economics.

My major sources of influence have been John Kenneth Galbraith, Joseph Stiglitz and Paul Krugman. I like their sharp analysis and the way they debunk conventional wisdom. Galbraith in particular has shaped my views on welfare with his arguments on how modern corporations and bureaucratic power may seriously distort social outcomes and heighten income inequality. This is quite relevant to Singapore, and I am personally concerned about our lack of welfare benefits and the growing gap between 'elites' and 'non-elites'. Our inadequate social safety net for the elderly and disabled worries me; the Economist *described our process of seeking help as 'tiresome and humiliating', and I agree. I believe that our system has much room for improvement.*

I believe that public policy must be grounded in mathematical graft. Empirical evidence provides us with a basis for analysis – so our ideas do not stray too far from the truth. I look forward to studying Econometrics and using statistical tools to investigate data, as I enjoy statistical analysis and admire the elegance of equations. I am fascinated by natural experiments and randomized ones such as those by the Jameel Poverty Action Lab. They inspired me because measuring the impact of policies can help us to choose cost-effective ways to improve them. For example, providing small incentives for immunization improved the take-up rate by nearly 140%.

Observing real-life policy changes has also been intriguing. The recent slew of austerity measures, for instance, seems too harsh to me: the Eurozone's growth has stagnated and the UK and US are facing the threat of a double-dip recession. Perhaps Martin Wolf is right when he argues that the UK should gradually reduce its debt, rather than slashing its budget by an unrealistic saving-spending ratio of GBP 5:1.

My interest in Europe's economies prompted me to organise the 1st European Union Youth Forum in Singapore. During this forum, we discussed issues ranging from the Eurozone debt crises to immigration and regional integration. I also took the chance to debate the crises' impact on Asia with the Chief Economist of Credit Suisse, and the viability of regional integration with the Head of the EU Delegation. This sparked my interest in trade, as I had to consider the effects of interdependence on an economy: vulnerability or resilience.

When I was at the Economic Research Institute of ASEAN to deliver a presentation on the ASEAN Youth Convention I organised, I was intrigued by the other proposals for economic cooperation: cross-border supply chain integration; public-private partnerships; and infrastructural development. Industrial policy in Asia has been generally successful; this may be attributed to how the government encourages the growth of sectors rather than specific companies.

I would also like to study the internet industry, which is revolutionising commerce. I recently started a study on blogshops to learn how blog owners establish credibility, manage risk, etc; I plan to continue this after A-levels. Europe's welfare systems are an interesting study; I look forward to comparing them to Singapore's. In future, I would like to conduct economic research and use statistical analysis to develop public policy. Singapore's welfare system is a significant concern for me, so I would pursue this notion of social justice.

I have a fast pace of working, but I sustain myself with a passion for the arts. I love watching theatre and musical performances, and I feel excited by the prospect of visiting the Globe. I am also a huge fan of Agatha Christie and Anthony Trollope – they have inspired in me a love of reading and an interest in British culture, and make me want to study in the UK.

Analysis

What makes this Personal Statement special is the personal tone and honesty it conveys. The opening paragraph is strong and has immediate impact. In only three sentences, the student effectively introduced who she is, how she understands the subject, and why she wants to study it, giving readers immediate insight into her background. The body of the text cleverly intertwines her knowledge and readings on the subject with her own analysis and opinions. She is able to convey that she can exert her own views based on informed knowledge and understanding on what she has read and experienced, which makes her Personal Statement stand out from those who simply list readings or other people's ideas. She incorporates many examples of her skills and experiences; the important thing here is that she effectively tailors them to her interest in Economics. However, the ending could be improved on as it is not as impactful as the rest of her Personal Statement.

Joon Hyung Kwon (Economics)

I was attending the Financial Maths Day organised by Goldman Sachs when Lehman Brothers collapsed. Back then I did not know why the Financial Crisis occurred or what it meant, but I certainly knew that I had the desire to find out. That gave me the passion to study Economics at university.

Due to my interest in the 2008 Financial Crisis, I wrote an essay by the title 'Are Recessions Inevitable?' for this year's Young Economist of the Year Essay Competition, which was highly commended, placing me in the top fifty in the country. During the research on this topic, I soon became fascinated by financial crises in general after reading The Return of Depression Economics *by Paul Krugman and* Globalization and Its Discontents *by Joseph Stiglitz. I concluded that recessions were inevitable due to unpredictable economic shocks, the increasing interconnectedness of the world economy, and the political inconvenience of predicting bad times ahead. As a result, I came to respect Economics for its constant struggle to understand the complex workings of economic systems.*

I would also like to study Economics for patriotic reasons. In my research into financial crises, the 1997 Asian Financial Crisis in particular grabbed my attention due to my childhood memories of economic trouble in my country, South Korea. I soon began to take interest in South Korea's rapid growth from absolute poverty to affluence within one generation. The pace of change and improvement in my home country never fails to fascinate me. I thoroughly enjoyed this research because I knew that I was now enjoying the fruits of that growth. I currently have an acute desire to return to my home country with much greater economic knowledge because I would then be in a position to aid its development.

I also learned from my research that the nature of economic growth is affected by the country's culture, history, politics and even religion. As a result, I realised that studying Economics would enable me to analyse many aspects of human behaviour. I would also like to interact fluently with the world's leading economies. Hence I am currently learning Mandarin and French. I write regularly for the school magazine on economic topics and assiduously take part in school debates. In addition, I was recently chosen to represent my school for the 2010 Singapore Young Leaders' Summit, which would be an opportunity to discuss economic issues.

I love analysing economic data. I am captaining my school team in entering the Bank of England 2.0 Interest Rate Challenge this year. I enjoyed every moment of reading through the Financial Times, *the* Economist, *the ONS figures, and the minutiae of MPC meetings for economic data and patterns. Moreover, after attending lectures and tutorials at LSE and Oxford, I observed that Economics is very mathematical. The tutorial on Game Theory, for example, contained a copious amount of Maths, which I relished learning. This experience spurred me on in studying Further Maths and Statistics. Economics has a double charm: the precise mathematical and statistical analysis coupled with the study of human behaviour.*

I carry out a lot of academic society work at school, currently chairing the school Mathematical Society and organizing trips to lectures outside school. I would like to carry on my society work at university, by forming a Korea Development Society. I was awarded the Lower Sixth prize for Economics at my school as well as the Harvard Prize which is given annually to only 100 Lower Sixth students in the country. I have been awarded music as well as academic scholarships, and lead the cello section in the school orchestra. I am also a keen cross-country runner, currently training for a twenty-mile charity run.

I want to understand how an economic system functions in the real world. I would like to help my country develop in our global age. I believe that studying Economics at university is the best way of fulfilling that ambition.

Analysis

By instantly 'locating himself in history', Joon helps create an impression of himself as having long been clued-up about economic current affairs. Some would find this expository paragraph effective, but it might be found a little pat by others; overall, his specificity is quite refreshing. Joon quickly establishes his academic credentials, which are impressive: making the Top 50 in Young Economist of the Year is worthy of note. Professing patriotism in a Personal Statement as a motive for studying a degree is a rare thing, and his elaboration is refreshing as well as poignant. His having written for his school magazine shows enthusiasm, as does his participation in debates. By the time he begins talking about chairing the school Maths Society, captaining his school team in the Interest Rate Challenge, representing his school in Singapore, and winning the coveted Harvard Prize, it is clear that Joon is a gifted candidate, shown by obvious enthusiasm and a surprising amount of impressive achievements that are connected to his chosen degree.

Minh Ngoc Nguyen (Politics, Psychology and Sociology)

I was born in Hanoi during one of the most important years of Vietnamese history: the initiation of the 'Open Door' policy, marking the shift from a state-controlled economy to a market one. My family experienced the effects of this change and, as I grew up, I was constantly reminded of my good fortune and the importance of compassion, humanity and social responsibility. I saw how economic development could increase the gap between rich and poor and resolved that when I grew up, I would do something to help society develop in ways that could benefit less fortunate people. In school, I learned to become active in my community through aid campaigns for Central Vietnam and working for a volunteer organisation to sponsor children's education. I also participated in extra-curricular activities such as working with the Hanoi International Theatre Society. Through this, I developed communication and leadership skills. I was able to enhance these skills when I attended the Global Young Leaders' Conference in July 2007. At this Conference, I was introduced to the international dimension of issues of social responsibility and global concerns such as genocide, gender inequality in Africa and the Kyoto Protocol. I also gained some understanding of the roles played by international institutions such as the United Nations and the ways in which youth empowerment could be a force for change. I was unaware at the time that this opportunity for cultural exchange and interaction with young leaders of my age would help me greatly in preparing for my experience at Pearson College.

Coming to Pearson College, I learned to become independent, to adapt to new environments and to understand the importance of cultural understanding in conflict resolution. Here I was introduced to concepts of sustainability and 'green economies', their potential for creating change in society and their present limited effectiveness.

Learning from my experiences at Pearson College, I began to notice changes in my country when I returned home this summer. I saw the tremendous effect that inflation and the food crisis had on people's daily lives. I noticed the ongoing transition from a traditional community-centred lifestyle to an individual-based, commercial one. Despite this, I also noticed the government's efforts to raise environmental awareness in urban citizens. I wanted to create an opportunity for others of my age to share in and discuss our knowledge of these local and global concerns. With four friends, I organised the Vietnam Youth Forum where thirty young Vietnamese discussed preservation of Vietnamese culture, sustainability, climate change, the Vietnamese economy in the global spectrum and the importance of community service. I was inspired by the opinions and talents of my peers and their resolution to make a difference in Vietnam. Through this Forum, I realised the importance of raising public awareness of these issues, and the roles of organisations and government in the policy-making necessary to face up to them. I want to understand how governments, pressure groups and individuals can be helped to take on the responsibility of dealing with the global challenges of my generation and, in particular, how all this can be achieved in a developing country, like Vietnam, with limited resources and technology.

For this, I need some in-depth knowledge and practical understanding of the workings of societies and the causes and inter-connection of global issues. A study of Social Political Science, Sustainable Development and Environmental Policies will provide me with the foundation on which to acquire this knowledge. Through these disciplines I also hope to develop the critical skills necessary to achieve my ambitions. These ambitions revolve around my fervent wish to contribute towards the change –environmental, political and social – that is necessary in my country. Studying at one of the best universities will be a major asset in my pursuit of this goal.

Analysis

Structurally, this Personal Statement could be a little stronger – three lengthy paragraphs could have been divided up more thematically, making for more lucid reading. Nevertheless, her opening statement is effective because it roots us in Nguyen's past without resorting to clichés. Her observations at a younger age of some of the consequences of economic growth demonstrate a keen mind, while her charitable side is proven by her involvement in aid campaigns. Most impressive is her attendance at the Global Young Leaders' Conference, showing that she has confidence, practical empathy and sensitivity to be savvy to global issues. Upon returning home to Vietnam, she was able to apply theoretical knowledge to a real socio-political situation; this skill is crucial for a successful PPS degree. Perhaps this obviously earnest and intelligent candidate could have mentioned a book or two that she had read. However, she has had practical experience, and seems dedicated to and driven by her subject as well as wider issues.

Natural Sciences

Mark Nicholson (Chemistry)

Imagine the world in 100 years' time; a world unrecognisable as our own, changed forever by a myriad of advances in science and technology. We could have evolved into a space-faring civilisation, or perhaps a society where genetically modified creatures aid our every footstep. We simply cannot know what the future holds; yet whatever it is, I want to help found the next era of innovation. I want to become a scientist.

For me, this dream began back at the age of eight, when I started reading The Dorling Kindersley Science Encyclopedia with my father. A year later, we had managed to go from cover to cover, giving me a basic grounding in science. Ever since, I have tried to find out more, with subscriptions to a children's science magazine and, more recently, the New Scientist. These have widened my scientific horizons, showing me subject areas I never knew existed, such as the rapidly developing world of nanotechnology, and allowing me to connect the separate subjects taught in school.

Winning Imperial College's Centenary Science Competition for Schools 2007 took me one step closer to my goal of being a scientist. As the lead entrant of our team of five, I led the presentation to over a hundred professors and students, and coordinated the writing of the essay which gained our place in the final. The experience was exhilarating, if nerve-wracking, and the research for the project stretched my mind beyond anything I had previously experienced. To continue stretching myself, I have started an Open University course called Discovering Science, which has so far proved very useful by teaching me how to study entirely on my own. The coursework has also started to hone my scientific writing skills, which will be very useful in later life.

In the business world, I have gained a week's work experience at Foster Wheeler, working as an assistant to chemical engineers. I really enjoyed the work they set, involving tracing the paths of chemicals through their plant and checking the interactive 3D simulation of the plant, which was fascinating as well as informative. The week was also good teamwork experience, as I had to work with all the chemical engineers on the project. I have had two other business-related experiences, one as Managing Director of a Young Enterprise company, and another on a two-day Challenge-of-Management course, on which I was also elected as the Director.

A gruelling World Challenge trek up Mount Kilimanjaro in 2006 defined, for me, the meaning of the word 'determination'. We reached the summit after four days of trudging up the slopes, culminating in a fifteen-hour walk which required no small amount of willpower and dedication, plus physical fitness. Playing tennis helped my fitness, as I currently play for my local club in the under-eighteens team, of which I am captain, and in the senior teams, as well as for the school. I would like to carry this hobby on at University, and pick up as many more pastimes as I can.

I believe I am ready for the next stage of my education. University will be the place to fulfil my dreams to helping mankind achieve its potential by furthering *our understanding of the world around us, whether the chemistry of the earth beneath our feet or mechanisms which make the universe tick. As a committed and able student, I am determined to contribute to University as a whole, in both academic and social circles, and so achieve my ultimate aim; to become a scientist.*

Analysis

Mark begins with a creative opening which is interesting to read. By not focusing on himself but, rather, focusing on the subject he wants to study, he reinforces his passion for it. The conclusion is similarly strong because it finishes with a sense of drive and motivation to pursue his ambitions. Mark succeeds in emphasizing the skills he takes away from each experience he describes. He writes eloquently but, at times, this eloquent rhetoric makes him come across as less believable. Especially combined with the big dreams and ambitions he outlines, too much rhetoric risks giving the impression that they are just empty words.

Overall, the Personal Statement is well structured with a natural flow both within and between paragraphs. Moreover, the student's eagerness to learn comes through well in this Personal Statement, due to his use of examples to demonstrate cases in which he has taken the initiative to 'find out more' about his subject.

Catherine Pulman (Biology)

When I read the biography of Francis Crick at fifteen, I was intrigued by the journey he had taken from physics to genetics. It was at this time that I realised a career in science was right for me. An avid reader of popular science, having now read most of the local library's biological sciences collection, I am enthused by a diverse range of topics and authors which stemmed from a discovery of Richard Dawkins' views on evolution. I am particularly attracted to the field of genetics, and it was perhaps Matt Ridley's Genome which really alerted me to the huge implications of such research. This area of science excites me not least because of its unending possibilities in research and development, but also because of the sheer sense of awe that its complexity and logic inspire. The discovery of the world of genetics was, for me, life-changing, and I am now enjoying tutoring the subject to a home-educated fifteen-year-old.

William Calvin's speculations on brain development in How Brains Think led me to consider the interesting connection between memory and obsessive-compulsive disorder. Having sent the author an e-mail about my thoughts, his reply prompted me to find out more about balanced polymorphisms, to which he suggested the connection was due. Menno Schilthuizen's Frogs, Flies and Dandelions and an article in New Scientist on epigenetics, combined with some thought-provoking observations in the fields whilst walking the dog, led me to investigate the development of four-leaf clovers over the summer. As I tried to understand the science behind the phenomenon, I found myself making use of several different scientific fields. It is this broad scientific understanding which I feel is so essential in a research career, and one which I believe a degree in Natural Sciences would lay down so well.

Earlier this year I was offered work experience with a local company which is developing a nucleic acid rapid diagnostic assay for Chlamydia. Over the few days that I spent with them, I learnt the basics of their technology, following an experiment through from cell culture to detection. I found the experience fascinating, and was delighted to return for four weeks in the summer. The lab-based research included investigations into probe stability, serovar inclusivity, and the relative merits of genomic versus plasmid DNA. Such work required logical thinking, careful planning, and a constant awareness of the dangers of contamination. I was also required to produce a presentation on market competitors and a report on the statistics of STDs worldwide. Working with a team of scientists in a business environment opened my eyes to the excitement, tension and competition involved in the industry, while confirming my conviction that this is just what I want in a future career.

I find the competitive nature of scientific research, and the debate it stimulates, highly motivating. As a keen debater of the school's Model United Nations team, I have attended six conferences and chaired two at St Laurence. I hope to be able to use and develop such skills both at University and during my future career. Aside from science, I am active in the community, both as a member of St John Ambulance *and the local Youth Council, and at school I mentor a Year 10 student. Last October, I was one of fifteen students from Wiltshire to attend the International Leadership Conference in Hong Kong, which involved workshops in leadership skills, and culminated in a group presentation for which our team was awarded second prize. In my spare time I enjoy French film and Oscar Wilde.*

Just as Crick had not a clue where his future career would lie as he embarked on his physics degree in 1934, I hope that during my time at University I, too, will discover areas of science more fascinating and exciting than any I have been exposed to thus far. It is for this reason that I hope to be considered to study Natural Sciences.

Analysis

More convincing than having read Francis Crick's biography at fifteen is Catherine's apparently comprehensive perusal of her local library's biology collection. Her Personal Statement is full of specific ideas from books and journals, and it is obvious that she has mastered many aspects of her subject. Her hunger for learning is obvious: not many students would have the curiosity to email a writer with their ideas, and to take the writer's response as a springboard for further learning. Her having been inspired when walking her dog suggests a propensity for thinking about scientific complexities in everyday life (and it adds a little humour as well). Catherine's tutoring of a school pupil shows an ability to help others academically. Her work experience with 'a team of scientists in a business environment' is an asset to her application. Her penultimate paragraph is effective in its concision and because of the high level of the attainments, while her concluding paragraph nicely ties up the Statement by bringing it all back to Crick.

Siddharth Jain (Biology)

The study of science is about the search for absolute truth. However, science is not like maths: there is no such thing as absolute certainty, rather degrees of probability. Arthur Koestler once said, 'The progress of science is strewn, like an ancient desert trail, with the bleached skeletons of discarded theories which once possessed eternal life.' What this illustrates to me is how the study of science is an evolving process, posing new questions on a daily basis. My affiliation to, and interest in science derives from my persistent desire to comprehend the world around me. Biology is the study of life, entailing all living organisms and life processes. Whether it be breeding high-protein strains of cassava or unfurling the genetic code in search of genes causing obesity, the study of life is not only fascinating but has ever-growing applications. My interest in epigenetic inheritance systems stems from a lecture by Susan Greenfield on Neuroplasticity at the Royal Institution. I find the concept of environmental factors suppressing gene activity intriguing and plan to present a paper for the School's science prize on this.

Choosing to do my Extended Essay in Biology has given me the opportunity to undertake the process of falsification of a chosen hypothesis. Whilst volunteering in Indian rural areas, I found not only severe malnutrition, but abundant cases of fungal infections; I decided to investigate the most effective commercially available yeast fungicide. By preparing agar plates inoculated with Candida utilis, I was able to test the efficacy of a range of fungicides. Contrary to my hypothesis, tea tree oil, a herbal remedy, was far more effective than all pharmaceutical fungicides; this was an illustrative example to me that science is unpredictable. Nature's enigmatic ways were further revealed to me whilst writing my Peterhouse Kelvin Science essay, which was described as 'outstanding' by the College, reaching the final shortlist. Writing on whether 'Males are Parasitic upon Females', I primarily thought I'd be researching males' roles in primitive society but ended up concluding that males and females worked in synergy to deliver the optimum chances of gene perpetuation: the issue was centred around the offspring. I learnt that to gain true insight into a subject you have to read and think for yourself.

Excelling in a biological degree doesn't only require an interest in the subject, but also certain aptitudes. Completing D of E gold, teaching as an NCO in the RAF, and doing school tours have given me the skills necessary to cohere with a diverse range of people in different environments. Following these pursuits whilst training eight times a week with the school's 1st VIII required excellent time-management skills, which were put on test during IB1 examinations: I came top in all my higher level examinations and notably achieved 96% in Biology. I teach Year 8 scientists weekly; obtaining an academic scholarship at that age I appreciate how interesting it is to be pushed beyond the syllabus. This has been enriching, providing me with an opportunity to share my enthusiasm and develop my knowledge when posed with challenging questions. This required planning and initiative, qualities also reflected in my roles as chair of various societies such as

Harpur Science, French, Economics and IB Social. These leadership skills led to me being appointed as a School Monitor.

I'm going to University to take a step towards achieving my own potential through guidance from the most learned in their fields. When at a Genetics master class at Cambridge, Dr Phillip Oliver opened my eyes to the fact that scientists achieving Nobel prizes were just students with passion, and that we students could rise to this level. I'm not the next Tim Hunt, I'm not the next Charles Darwin; I aspire to be the first Siddharth Jain.

Analysis

Siddharth is an extremely passionate candidate. The opening statement displays originality but could be more concise, for example by cutting the obvious sentence that 'biology is the study of life...' Instead, Siddharth should more briefly describe his motivation before beginning a new paragraph that demonstrates his fields of interest (through attendance of lectures and submission of a paper for the school's science prize). Equally, Siddharth's closing statement is needlessly hyperbolic and therefore rather impersonal, verging on insincere. The applicant's real-life research experience in India is highly impressive as it displays motivation and a practical foundation for advanced research. Willingness to participate in competitions, submit extra-curricular essays and attend masterclasses demonstrates unusual enthusiasm and a solid basis for a degree in biology. Likewise, Siddharth does well to emphasise academic excellence. Finally, the candidate's extra-curricular achievements are especially impressive as he directly relates transferable skills gained – such as time management, planning and initiative, leadership skills, and so on – to the study of his chosen subject.

Indranil Banik (Physics)

Ever since my earliest years, I have been fascinated by the wonders of the universe. My interest in Physics stems from the early realisation that it is this discipline which holds the key to understanding these phenomena. I am fascinated by ideas like the expanding universe and extraterrestrial life. I have carefully followed numerous space missions as these provide insights into the workings of the universe as well as being remarkable in their own right, especially when they go to other planets. This is the unique aspect of our time: that we can not only speculate about the universe but empirically prove certain theories about it.

Many years ago I looked at Mars with a telescope. It was much closer to Earth and so it looked enormous. I even saw its icy polar caps. This opened my eyes to the wonders of worlds outside our own. NASA then launched two Rover missions to Mars which I have followed very closely. Their discoveries and pictures are truly stunning. I also saw the rings of Saturn and the space station's shiny solar arrays slowly rotating, a testament to our technological prowess. I visited the National Space Centre in Leicester where I saw rocks brought back from the Moon. I also visited the NASA Kennedy Space Centre where I climbed the launch pad and for a moment felt like the Apollo astronauts. The technology seems almost as amazing as the actual science.

I grew up with Scientific American *and* National Geographic *because my parents have been subscribing to them for many years. I enjoy reading many of their articles, especially on energy technology and cosmology. This led me to enter the Combat Climate Change competition twice. In one, I proposed using hydrogen as the main carrier of energy. I also entered the Science Prize Competition with an essay on the evidence for dark matter and experimental methods for producing and detecting it. These both required a lot of independent research.*

I have been fascinated by the origin of the cosmic microwave background radiation so I am excited to think that the Planck satellite has just started to measure it with unprecedented accuracy. This should help test exciting new cosmological theories like the cyclic model and inflation, as well as measure the amount of dark matter. I also enjoyed reading a fascinating tale of string theory's development in The Elegant Universe *by Brian Greene and of a mission that forever changed our understanding of water on Mars in* Exploring Mars *by Steve Squyres.*

As I was always strong in Mathematics, I did my Maths GCSE and A-levels on my own two years early, requiring me to learn a lot of totally new concepts. I have won a gold medal for being in the top forty nationwide in the 2008 Olympiad Maclaurin Paper and a Certificate of Distinction in the British Mathematical Olympiad in 2009 by doubling my previous year's score in it. I also participated in the UKMT Team Maths Challenges in Years 8 and 9, using both teamworking skills as well as mathematical ones. All of these challenges require a great deal of lateral thinking. As well as the BMO in December, I plan to do the Physics Olympiad in November 2009.

I enjoy playing tennis and have represented my school in cricket. There, I volunteered as a Peer Mentor in Year 10. In July, I was elected a senior prefect. Among my responsibilities are helping the office, monitoring other prefects and liaising with parents. This has reinforced to me the importance of teamwork and organisation. I am a member of the school's debating society and have won all of my debates so far. This has improved my public speaking and thinking skills. During my work experience, I polished my communication skills. I look forward to learning Astrophysics at the highest level as part of my degree and beyond and using it to explain many complex and interesting phenomena. I relish the challenges that this will bring.

Analysis

This is a strong Personal Statement, containing clearly defined paragraphs and striking a good balance of academic and extra-curricular achievement. Indranil's writing style is concise and clearly demonstrates interest in the particular field of Astrophysics. Discussing this specialty in depth at the interview stage will appear impressive. This candidate is able to demonstrate his enthusiasm for Astrophysics beyond his A-levels through visits to space centres and entering science competitions. He could have further discussed his work experience. The applicant also shows an awareness of recent scientific developments and reading materials in the field, demonstrating readiness to push himself. Additionally, his direct and specific list of academic merits is excellent. However, the first two paragraphs both discuss his background in Astrophysics, and could be condensed to discuss further the scientific theory which better exemplifies academic talent. Colloquial phrases such as 'a lot of' could be replaced by more sophisticated words like 'substantial', since his language is too simplistic at times.

Emma Shaw (Biology)

A World Challenge expedition to Central America was the catalyst that really ignited my passion for Biology and the Life Sciences. I became particularly fascinated by the extraordinary diversity of species in the Belizean jungle and my desire to learn more about the evolutionary theory behind this diversity has grown ever since. The 'Nucleic Acids' module at school barely even scraped the surface of what is, to me, a totally mind-boggling topic. The concept of a single chemical being the common genetic foundation for all life on Earth completely astounds me; if we are merely 'gene transporters', why do we exhibit such phenotypic variation?

After receiving Genome, *a book by Matt Ridley, for my birthday I have realised that this area of Biology is an ever-expanding black hole of questions and theories and it has become my goal to find some answers. The most intriguing part of the book for me was the theory of the RNA world and the Last Universal Common Ancestor, as I have never come across such exciting concepts before. The simplicity with which Ridley discusses what is essentially the foundation of life, chromosome by chromosome, really opened my eyes to a different way of thinking. One part of the book in particular made me question; am I really just a mass of cells, each one competing to further their genetic content for the good of themselves? I have since started reading* The Selfish Gene *by Richard Dawkins, which seems to focus on this rather bleak biological concept, though from a slightly different perspective.*

In July I was selected to study Biology at the Eton College Universities' Summer School, where I spent ten intensive days covering many new aspects of Biology. Although the lessons were often challenging, the style of the course gave me a real taster for University life and has only strengthened my ambition to pursue a career in Science.

Thanks to my many extra-curricular interests, my organisational skills have always been exceptional. I have always managed to juggle a number of activities outside of school, whilst remaining very committed to my school work. I have recently completed my Grade 8 in Classical Ballet, which has required a vast amount of dedication and discipline over the last fourteen years. I also enjoy playing the piano and have previously taught younger children on a part-time basis. Having just completed my Gold expedition during the summer, I really feel that the Duke of Edinburgh's Award is one which is hugely rewarding and beneficial to young people, so I have therefore decided to volunteer on a weekly basis to support other students who are participating in the Bronze and Silver Award schemes.

I am a firm believer in learning through experience and constantly try to find new ways of pushing the boundaries, both academically and personally. After my expedition last summer, I have definitely caught the 'Travel Bug' and am planning to take a Gap Year to complete more humanitarian and conservation work. A particular highlight in Guatemala was working at ARCAS, a conservation centre caring for animals injured by the illegal trafficking trade, and I hope to spend far more time helping such organisations. Not only will a year abroad equip me with invaluable life skills and experiences, but it will feed my hunger to learn as much as possible about the world around me. Getting out there really makes Science jump from a page in a textbook into real life and I have no doubt that the scientific baggage I collect on my travels will fuel me through many more years of academic study.

Analysis

Emma displays enthusiasm as well as evidence of pursuing the subject outside regular schoolwork, and excels in demonstrating extra-curricular dedication. The applicant's experience in Belize for the World Challenge is both memorable and impressive, as is her rejection of her schoolwork as 'barely scraping the surface', expressing the desire to take the subject to a much deeper level. However, only half of the Personal Statement directly discusses the subject; the applicant should instead focus more intently on Biology, including aspects of her academic work that inspire her, or her reading of Dawkins. She could also discuss rather less well-known works to appear more diverse in her knowledge. Her language is eloquent and sophisticated, although the candidate occasionally wastes words in an already short statement, including the phrases 'for my birthday' and 'a book'. The application appears somewhat constructed and clichéd at times, such as the way she refers to the Duke of Edinburgh's Award, reading Dawkins and over-emphasizing her gap year. It is therefore made less impressive than the more *personal* insight and passion evident in other candidates' Statements.

Jessica Denman (Pharmacology)

Science is a way to satisfy my curiosity as it creates a means to explore into the unknown. The use of science to solve biological diseases and pain relief in humans particularly intrigues me. I am fascinated by the complexity of the human body and the intricate mechanisms involved which need to be unravelled to identify the process of disease, so a cure can be developed to enhance human health.

GCSEs challenged my learning and fuelled my passion for science through fascinating concepts which exposed everyday biological processes. This drove me to achieve Outstanding Achievement awards for all my science subjects and the Highest Achievement Award for the year. I thrived at the progression to A-level as my studies became science focused and the concepts became more advanced.

My enthusiasm for science has led me to explore the subject beyond the curriculum. I independently studied the Open University course, Molecules, Medicines and Drugs: a Chemical Story, *alongside my A-levels. I found studying drug development and other content captivating and I desired to study the subject to a greater depth. This decision was finalised by research into pharmaceutical companies and their innovative R&D projects into an array of diseases. In addition, access to the OU Library, gained through the course, has been beneficial allowing me to follow up my interests by reading* New Scientist *eJournals about current scientific advances.*

My future in science was confirmed after attending an Evolution East Midlands Annual Sixth Form Conference. I was inspired by the passion and enthusiasm expressed in the talks presented by innovative professionals from a wide variety of biosciences. Their energy was contagious and made me anticipate my future in science and what I hoped to achieve – to advance scientific knowledge.

I have had the privilege to experience pioneering research first hand by carrying out a 5-week Nuffield Science Bursary Project over the summer. The project, undertaken in the Human Genetics Laboratory at the University of Nottingham, was to help the department's research into Alzheimer's disease genetic biomarkers by developing a method to obtain sufficient material from the potential candidate gene TRIM15 for deep resequencing. During the project, I substantially developed my experimental skills by performing DNA extraction, whole-genome amplification, Polymerase chain-reaction optimisation and DNA visualisation using electrophoresis. The project also developed my scientific writing and communication skills by producing a report and presenting a poster of my experience. Working as part of a team with the pioneering scientists at the forefront of science was an incredible experience which advanced my biological knowledge and showed me the unpredictability of research which makes it so fascinating.

By undertaking a Physical Science Summer School at Nottingham University, I got a taste of university life. Living on campus for the week, I experienced academic sessions combined with a huge array of social activities – it was definitely a routine that suited my personality!

My persistence and motivation for everything I do are shown not only by my grades but through my ability to balance a part-time waitress job and commitment to equestrianism alongside my A-levels. My part-time job allows me to effectively work as part of a team, practise courteous communication skills and remain composed under pressure. I am a competitive, adventurous and determined individual; this personality enabled me to complete the 180-mile Pembrokeshire Coast walk.

I look forward to the challenges that a science degree will present and hope to continue my study post-university with the intent to pursue a career in pioneering research to advance scientific knowledge.

Analysis

Despite her slightly bland style, Jessica manages effectively to convey a genuine, consistent interest in pharmacology – not only did she gain 'high achiever' awards during her GCSEs, but took an Open University course alongside her A-levels. Her thin dossier of extra-curricular activities is more than compensated for by her subject-focused involvements outside of the school. The 'East Midlands Conference' is an example of this, but better examples – showing her actual skill and competence rather than just her enthusiasm – follow. Her Nuffield Science Project is particularly impressive, partly because of its length and partly because she participated in experimentation and research. It helps that she really goes into detail, mentioning 'TRIM15' and explicitly delineating her responsibilities, which shows that she maintains a good sense of the importance of her contributions. With such solid academic and scientific credentials, it's totally understandable that she doesn't dwell too much on extra-curricular activities.

James Kellett (Chemistry)

My desire to study chemistry further was initially fired up by a keen longing to understand biology at a sub-cellular level. In my biology lessons and reading, I soon came to realise that biology was almost completely based on chemistry; and hence that chemistry, although being a stimulating mental exercise in itself, was also the basis for all life and technology. From then on I was hooked. I have recently done a research project and given a talk on monoclonal antibodies, which although currently produced with a biological method, will hopefully be industrially synthesised by a chemical method in the future, making them more widely available. I am also interested in physics and this interest was rewarded by a top ten in the country score at GCSE physics, followed more recently by a score of 298/300 in AS. I intend to take Olympiad and AEA papers in both physics and chemistry this year and look forward to the challenges they will present. I have read sections from The Magic Universe *by Nigel Calder, on the Higgs Boson, the possibility of wormholes and how the enzyme telomerase can be used to prevent ageing, effectively giving immortality. I know that most of these topics are far beyond our current technology, but they are scientifically feasible and, after my degree, I would love to be part of a research team that investigates some of this world-changing science. I read* New Scientist *and enjoy the debate over particles, but I am really looking forward to the turning on of the LHC which offers the possibility of allowing current debate to resolve on one grand theory.*

I have done three work experience placements. My first was in an international Private Equity firm in London, which helped me to get an idea both of how the business world works and also what life would be like in that career. More recently I have worked as a tennis coach, which helped to give me a perspective of what a less formal job is like. The highlight of my summer was winning a placement at a GSK R&D site. I found it to be a very stimulating environment in which university-level chemistry is applied. It was amazing to see how chemists and engineers worked together in a myriad of teams to contribute to the final product, demonstrating to me how important and exciting the overlap between physics and chemistry is. I helped perform factor screening using lab automation technology, effectively performing 20 experiments simultaneously with the computer logging results. I feel this kind of technology will help individual research chemists become much more effective, since an experiment which would take a whole week manually can be left to run itself over a weekend, allowing the chemist to spend much more time on analysis.

In my free time I am a keen actor, sportsman and debater. I have been in numerous school plays including a modern performance of 'Tis Pity She's a Whore which was reviewed by the NSDF. I have also led and directed a performance of Julius Caesar *for the SYF. I have gained good management skills from directing as well as an aptitude for public speaking and presentations from acting. I am an enthusiastic tennis player, representing the school in the Second Six as well as playing club tournaments. I also enjoy off-piste skiing and intend to take my level*

1 instructor course later this year. Although not in a top rugby team, I get pleasure from participating in inter-school matches, savouring the camaraderie and team spirit. I am the secretary of the debating society, which is entering the Mace competition this year. I enjoy putting my leadership skills to use as a corporal and qualified weapons instructor in the CCF, leading a section of eight 15-year-olds. I also provide service and leadership to my school and house as a house prae.

I entered Tonbridge as an academic scholar and have always applied myself in academic work and extra-curricular activities; and I hope to continue doing so at one of the country's great institutions of learning.

Analysis

The introduction kicks off with some big, interesting claims about the influence of chemistry, which makes this student's Personal Statement impressive. The student can expect interviewers to ask questions based on these claims and will therefore find it useful to prepare an oral explanation as to exactly why, for instance, he believes 'biology was almost completely based on chemistry', since this is not explained in the Personal Statement. He uses many technical terms, which helps to show his understanding for his subject and his commitment to learning more about it. The Personal Statement also shows that he is driven and keen to accept new challenges. The student incorporates examples of work experience, of which the first two are less relevant to his subject than the third, but would still be useful to include if only he expanded more on the skills he had learnt from the experience. The same critique applies to the extra-curricular interests section.

Andrew Wedlake (Physical Science)

I have found studying all of my A-level subjects fascinating and have found choosing just one to specialise in very difficult, so the opportunity offered by the Natural Sciences course to continue to study all of them makes it perfect for me. I would like to improve my understanding of the scientific world by studying a broad range of scientific disciplines as opposed to narrowing my mind, which is constantly full of curiosity, by only specialising in one subject. For me, the main draw of science is that it explains how and why everything in the world works. In a world where the boundaries between the scientific disciplines are becoming more and more superficial, I would relish the chance to gain the interdisciplinary knowledge that will help me to understand and explain as many things as possible. Having been part of a Natural Sciences Headstart course focusing in materials science at Cambridge, I have an idea about the structure of the Natural Science course: the flexibility and broadness of the topics studied makes the course very appealing to me.

As part of a team, I have studied and analysed data from NASA's Cassini-Huygens regarding the magnetosphere of one of Saturn's moons, Titan. This required an understanding of shock formation in non-collisional plasmas and gave me a taster of astrophysics, which I built on by researching meteorites and presenting my findings, once again as part of a team, to a professor at Imperial College, London. Both of these projects improved my ability to work in a team – a skill that I understand to be important in lab work and research. I undertook two weeks' work experience at ERA Technology, learning about the latest satellite technology as well as IT skills. At school, I have led experiments and talks at the physics open day for new students. This required presentation skills and the ability to clearly communicate at an appropriate level. I also needed these skills when I taught chemistry lessons to Year 6 students at a local primary school. Despite not continuing it beyond AS-level, I have maintained a strong interest in biology, having written reports on 'Marijuana as a Treatment for Glaucoma' amongst other topics. My scientific thirst is partly quenched by regularly reading New Scientist *along with stories from Internet websites, including the BBC site.*

My scientific skills have always been backed up by my mathematical interest and ability. I am a founding member of the school Mathematics Society, in which we explore more challenging mathematical concepts and questions, as well as a columnist in the school mathematics magazine. Furthermore, I have represented the school in numerous mathematical competitions: Hans Woyda (local interschool mathematics competition); Surrey School Mathematics Team Challenge, in which my team came 3rd; and the Senior Team Mathematics Challenge run by the UKMT. I have received at least a gold certificate in the UKMT Mathematics Challenge every year for the past 7 years and recently run mathematics and chemistry revision classes for schoolmates. I think this highlights my willingness to help my friends outside of scheduled lessons – a quality that will be vital at university.

I play trombone at a grade 7 standard and I am lead trombone in two bands. I have been on four separate tours in Europe with these bands playing at large venues. I have achieved distinction at grade 5 music theory. I play tennis regularly, as well as playing for one of the school football teams. I also coach football to 13–15-year-olds and have volunteered to help teach 10–13-year-olds at my local church's Sunday school. I have completed the Duke of Edinburgh's Bronze Award, which required team-working skills.

Being able to do all of the above on top of 5 AS-levels shows my ability to manage my time – a skill that will prove vital in my years at university.

Analysis

Andrew's strength shows in his repeated demonstrations of his evident passion for Science through extra-curricular, subject-specific activities – his projects relating to NASA and Imperial College are highly impressive. The candidate furthers this by emphasizing specific knowledge and interpersonal skills acquired, but could elaborate on the academic ramifications of such projects. His application is strengthened by a clear talent and enthusiasm for Mathematics, reinforced by founding a Mathematics society and writing for a Mathematics magazine. His interconnected academic and extra-curricular success also displays commitment, enthusiasm and time-management skills.

The candidate could condense his opening paragraph, which becomes repetitive. Equally, phrases like 'more and more' could be shortened to 'increasingly' to save space. The final sentences could be more relevant and concise, and might be improved by ending with a sentence summarizing his approach to and passion for to the subject.

Michael Ashford (Physics)

Physics studies the foundations of the universe, giving us a deeper understanding of the world in which we live and managing to explain the incredible complexities of the cosmos with relatively simple equations and principles. Physics attracts me as a subject because it is the most fundamental of the sciences. I savour the challenge of solving logical and mathematical problems, both of which are intrinsic aspects of physics.

I have enjoyed my A-level physics studies but I have found a greater stimulus and challenge in reading works by Feynman, Gleick and Hawking which have captivated my interest. Feynman's QED shocked me with the idea that many of the phenomena of the universe can be described as a result of just three basic actions: the movement of a photon, the movement of an electron and an electron emitting or absorbing a photon. I have become increasingly aware that some of the most basic scientific principles that I have always held to be true, such as the fact that light travels in straight lines, are not strictly accurate. Instead, the probabilistic wave function of the photon takes every possible path between two points. We do not observe this, however, because most paths other than the straight line paths cancel out. This book gave me an appreciation of the genius and creativity of the minds of the pioneers of QED and of their ability to think beyond our preconceptions and look at the world from an entirely different perspective.

After my AS exams, I completed a six-week physics project on special and general relativity with a partner, which we presented to the rest of the group. I really enjoyed being able to work outside the curriculum on more complicated and interesting material. I found that the notion of absolute time, which we seem to accept almost naturally, falls apart under the theory of relativity. I was particularly impressed when I discovered that such a significant area of physics can be demonstrated with simple examples and experiments, such as the number of muons detected at the Earth's surface.

Mathematics forms the backbone of physics, with much of it able to find an application in the subject. Taking Further Maths has allowed me to broaden my base of mathematical knowledge and develop a wider range of techniques. Last year I represented the school in the Senior Team Maths Challenge in which we were national finalists.

Currently I am Head Boy of my school, taking charge of a team of prefects to assist in the running of the school. I organise duty rotas for the prefects and represent the students at various social occasions. I am also leading a fundraising project for an extension to our sixth-form centre. These responsibilities have improved both my organisational and communication skills, as well as my ability to work under pressure, which are key components of university study.

I am second in charge of the school's CCF RAF section, helping to co-ordinate training and activities for around fifty cadets. Teamwork is vitally important in the CCF and a valuable skill which I have been able to develop. As part of my role, I teach the topic of propulsion to other cadets. Being able to share knowledge of a subject in which I have a genuine interest is something I have found very rewarding.

Outside school, I have practised kickboxing for the past eight years, receiving my black belt in 2005. I feel that through kickboxing I have been able to develop determination and discipline. I also cycle regularly and enjoy both the physical and mental challenge of long cycle rides.

I am looking forward to gaining a better understanding of the world by studying physics at degree level, where I will be able to explore topics which until now I have only touched on. My continual curiosity of how the world works gives me the desire to study the subject in depth and I am sure that I have the drive and enthusiasm necessary for the demands of a physics course.

Analysis

Michael's opening paragraph shows an understanding of the fundamentals and importance of physics, while stating exactly why Physics captivates him. He claims that non-curriculum reading has stimulated him more than his A-levels; a promising sign for a university applicant. Moreover, by showing how what he has learnt has challenged his conceptions of this subject, he shows an ability to revise his hypothesis, a valuable trait for a scientist. Michael's post-AS project further demonstrates his interest in the subject, which he backs up with examples of academic and extra-curricular achievements. His participation in the Senior Maths Challenge demonstrates his mathematical capabilities (obviously crucial to a Physics degree), while the responsibilities of being Head Boy and 2nd-in-command of his school's RAF section speak for themselves. Michael's final paragraph rounds off his Statement by reinforcing his love for the subject in an unforced way, and overall the reader is left with the impression of a confident, capable student with a real interest in Physics.

Engineering

Nick Wise (Mechanical/Industrial Engineering)

'The important thing is not to stop questioning...' – Albert Einstein.

I have always been interested in the world around me and how things work. I was and still am the student who continually asks 'Why?' From a young age I have found pleasure in maths and problem-solving and I believe that engineering can provide a challenging but rewarding future career that will continue to provide the conundrums on which I thrive.

In July 2007, I organised a week's work experience with Peter Brett Associates, a civil engineering consultancy firm in Reading that specialises in infrastructure projects. There I worked alongside qualified engineers on real projects, including the design of a new road junction and the flood defences being built to protect a new housing development. I found it very exhilarating to see my work making a difference in real-life situations. Through engaging with engineers, I developed invaluable problem-solving, team-working and time-management skills, whilst learning how to use CAD improved my computer literacy. I thoroughly enjoyed my time there and, at the end of the week, decided that I wanted to be an engineer.

It was my experiences at Peter Brett that galvanised me to do more, and at the start of my AS-levels, I applied for Headstart engineering, as I was keen to find out as much about engineering as I could. During the course at Cambridge, I attended lectures and conducted experiments. I particularly liked finding out about fluid dynamics and would like the chance to expand my knowledge on the subject. This course confirmed to me that I wanted to study engineering. I want to explore how the world works, and use that knowledge to solve problems that are real, not theoretical.

Maths and physics have always been a part of my life and I have represented my school at maths on numerous occasions, locally and nationally, both on my own and as part of a team for the UK team maths challenge. I'm fascinated by the wonders of physics, whether string theory and the standard model or black holes. As an avid reader, I seek to increase my knowledge on the subject and have read A Brief History of Time *by* Stephen Hawking, One, Two, Three, Infinity *by George Gamow and* The Music of the Primes *by Marcus Du Sautoy, as well as subscribing to* New Scientist *and being a regular reader of the* Engineering and Technology *magazine.*

I have a very active life outside of school. I have played the trombone for more than eight years and taught myself the piano over the past two. I hold grade 8 at the trombone and am principal trombonist of the Berkshire Youth Orchestra and Berkshire Youth Brass Band, as well as several other brass, wind and orchestral groups. Every Saturday morning I help out with a younger brass band, something I've been doing for several years now. I've found it really rewarding to watch the band, and particularly the trombone section whom I work with, to grow both musically and personally. I enjoy being a part of so many bands and the opportunities they give me to perform a variety of music in front of audiences in this country and abroad. Through music I have developed important leadership skills and a real understanding of the teamwork required to produce effective performances from a group of people. It also takes organisation and efficient time-keeping skills to fit my musical commitments around my school work and my part-time job as a cleaner, something which I believe I do well.

I believe that in engineering I have found a subject that will be a focus for my interests, whilst being challenging and rewarding in equal measure.

Analysis

Nick is clearly enthusiastic and shows dedication to studying engineering in numerous ways, building up solid foundations for a degree. His opening paragraph exemplifies his passion for the subject, and the Einstein quotation is a nice touch; however, the introduction could be shortened, since his only point is his inquisitive nature. The candidate's subsequent paragraphs describing his work experience and engineering courses are excellent; he balances subject-specific knowledge with transferable skills gained very well, as well as demonstrating several years' thought and practice behind his application. The applicant's additional reading is also very impressive, and could be elaborated on at interview to show his ability to handle degree-level study. Some phrases add little substance and take up unnecessary space, such as stating that the course 'confirmed that he wanted to study engineering', and repeatedly saying he 'wants to explore how the world works'. Finally, the candidate's extra-curricular section is too expansive.

Chloe Underdown (Civil and Environmental Engineering)

Although initially attracted to engineering by the thought of designing impressive structures such as the new Wembley Stadium, the Falkirk Wheel and the Millennium Bridge at Gateshead, I find myself increasingly drawn to the more essential services that engineers provide, such as the constant supply of clean water that we often take for granted. With the issue of climate change becoming ever more prominent, I hope that as an engineer I can help develop the world sustainably. A career in engineering appeals as it is varied and challenging, involves solving problems and is the practical application of maths and physics, subjects I have always enjoyed and where I feel my greatest abilities lie. The decision to study engineering was confirmed by two weeks of work experience in the structural engineering department at Waterman Partnership where I learnt how to draw some basic structural plans for current projects and shadowed senior engineers. It gave a great insight into what a structural engineer does on a daily basis, which I did not have previously.

More recently I took part in the Engineering Education Scheme. This involved working on a project entitled 'Variable Coloured Lighting for Vehicle Interior' in association with the Ford Motor Company. Taking part increased my electronics knowledge greatly and I thoroughly enjoyed designing a circuit to control the lighting. As well as the skills developed through working in a team, I also had a chance to improve my presentation skills when we presented our project to a team of assessors. For my contribution to the project, I received a BA Crest Award at Gold Standard. Similarly, I took part in a Headstart course where I was involved in activities from a range of engineering disciplines, including a research project in a small group which I then presented to the other students and the professors.

Within school I am a prefect and previously was a member of the CHIPS (Childline in Partnership with Schools) team. CHIPS is a peer support team for which I was trained by Childline and received a Diana Princess of Wales Memorial Award. I have also had the opportunity to take part in the Young Enterprise scheme and Duke of Edinburgh's Awards, which taught me the importance of good communication within a team. As an active member of Girlguiding, I am a member of a Ranger Unit where I regularly attend meetings. I have been a Young Leader at a Brownie unit for 4 years and am working towards my leadership qualification to become a Guider. I enjoy working with the girls and helping them to develop new skills has improved my patience. Recently I was selected to represent the UK on an international trip to New Zealand. It was a fantastic opportunity to meet Guides from all over the world as well as gain a greater understanding of New Zealand's culture and heritage.

I have chosen to defer entry in order to experience a range of opportunities outside of academia. The main part of my trip will be spent in South America where I will volunteer on two projects. Firstly in Peru, I will be working alongside Peruvian experts on archaeological sites restoring ancient Inca ruins. The Incas have interested me since I first heard about Machu Picchu and I hope to visit the famous site as well as the Inca capital Cusco. Secondly, in Chile, I will be working on a conservation project helping to construct a trail which will help preserve the forest and surrounding areas while still allowing visitors. Basic Spanish lessons will allow me to get to know people and places more fully. Following this, I will return to New Zealand to work and to travel through the South Island, which will allow me to gain invaluable skills and experiences. Travelling is something I have long wished to do and I believe I will return with greater maturity and independence ready for university.

Analysis

This candidate's eloquent and sophisticated Personal Statement is particularly rich in discussion of relevant work experience in engineering, giving her an edge. Her lack of detail about academic achievement is fine, since her grade information is contained in all the associated UCAS data. This applicant's main weakness is her failure to balance detail about engineering projects with directly relevant information; her introductory sentences contain little factual information, and the candidate could have elaborated on her interest in sustainable engineering. Likewise, she gives no detail on her 'research project' at Headstart, and explaining this would have been impressive. Over half of this Personal Statement discusses superfluous extra-curricular activities and her gap-year plans, which detracts from the application. The candidate could have related the skills gained from her extra-curricular activities to her career plans, such as teamwork, dedication and commitment.

Bryan Sin Kwok Wong (Technology)

Design, coupled with science, has appealed to me since childhood. I love the creative, visual as well as logical aspect of what I see – from the toy to the computer. It would be thrilling to, one day, be one of those to design the wonders of technology. I enjoy reading about science in Newsweek and on the Internet. Engineers are vital to progress; I believe electronics and bio/nanotechnology are the future of this ever-changing world. These fields, especially nanotechnology, have wide applications: drug delivery, prosthetics, novel structural materials – for vehicles or medical tools – and even quantum computing! My interest for engineering stems from my desire to help others and to improve life in my own way by designing systems at the nano-scale. I want to be one of those innovators venturing to change the world through the science of small things. An unconventional mindset is called for. It is exactly what is most alluring about engineering.

I aspire to study at the prestigious British Universities as graduates from England are inspiring, eminent figures. Their first-rate education is the reason behind their success. The more so, Mauritius being a former British Colony, the reputation of British Universities is well established on the island. As an islander, I dream to have access to higher education at reputable British institutions, to be thereby exposed to a different culture and able to view the world in a different light.

I believe that I have what it takes to study engineering. During the last years, I have had the chance to apply my skills – logic and rhetoric – via competitions such as the Model United Nations as reporter or the Australian Mathematics Competition, scoring a High Distinction in 2007. I also ranked eighth and tenth in Mauritius in Mathematics and Physics respectively at the O-level University of Cambridge Local Syndicate Examinations. Yet, I am most proud of the Design and Communication coursework I produced for my O-level Exams, which won me the 1st place at National Level. It shaped my ambition to exploit my creativity and help design innovative devices as an engineer.

Academics aside, I am a member of the 9th Lower Plaines Wilhems Scout Troop where my diligence was rewarded with the 'Best Performance' Award in 2006. I was promoted to 'Patrol Leader' that same year. As such, I was able to apply my management abilities and eventually lead an eight-man team to be elected 'Best Patrol'. Today, as the 'Scout Leader' of seventy boys, I am working on the blueprint for a Grand Concert, gathering over 400 people, for the Troop's 50th anniversary. My 7 years as Boy Scout taught me how to deal with others, work in teams, and pursue my dreams. I believe an engineer requires similar qualities to succeed.

Karate is my second passion. Practising the art since 2004 and now a brown belt, I learnt many things from my Shian – or teacher. He always used to say: 'From karate, we gain something priceless; this cannot be gained in any other discipline. We often fall but we stand up again, determined not to fall once again.' Karate procures me a philosophy of life that taught me self-discipline, perseverance and most of all, I learnt about myself. Nothing is taken for granted. What motivates me about engineering is that one has to take initiative. Engineers need to make things happen and solve real-life issues for a better world.

'When you do something, try your best. Otherwise, you are wasting your time.' My parents' credo compelled me to spend my leisure time as constructively as I can. For instance, after having played the flute as a child, I recently started guitar lessons to build on my music talents.

As an aspiring engineer, I have a dream: to initiate the next 'Google' success in product design. Pursuing tertiary education in engineering will not only fulfil a personal objective but also help me to contribute to the development of my country and, by extension, to return something to the world.

Analysis

Bryan appears keen in his opening paragraph, but besides voicing an attraction to nano-science, his interests – such as reading about science 'on the Internet', and wanting to 'help others' – wouldn't necessarily differentiate him from other candidates. His next paragraph reinforces his desire to succeed, but his third paragraph is his strongest, featuring an impressive array of achievements on the national level, both related and unrelated to engineering. Bryan's descriptions about experiences with the scout troops and karate are too long, and the section about his musical talents seems like an afterthought. His obvious ambition and impressive achievements substantiate his enthusiasm; however, greater concision, more cogent linking of points, and less reliance on quotes and clichés would have made this a stronger Personal Statement.

Kevin Surya Widjaja (Chemical Engineering)

My fascination with Chemical Engineering was inspired, in particular, by a seminar on world energy resources held by my high school in Indonesia, allowing me to discover the immense world demand on energy and our high dependency on fossil fuel. I aim to become a chemical engineer so that I can make a positive contribution to solve the energy crisis problem by exploring renewable energy.

Last summer, I had a great work experience involving the chemistry of petroleum with Lubrizol Ltd, a petroleum additive company in Derby, on a training programme, mainly in the chemical synthesis lab that has the facility to build star-shaped polymers. I learnt to use equipment such as the gas chromatograph, and I also learnt that to achieve the best outcome from experiments requires patience and discipline. This experience gave me a valuable insight and perspective on how a petrochemical company works. I also had a two-week training stint in a chemical plant in Indonesia, Styrindo Mono Indonesia, producing styrene monomers. I saw how chemical engineers work together as a group in a huge plant, creating new processes, troubleshooting, and improving the existing processes such as reducing heat loss and reusing the side product to give a better yield. Last summer ended with a training attachment in Cerestar Flourmill, Indonesia. Although the nature of a flourmill may appear to be very different from the chemical plant, I realise that the principles of both plant operations are the same.

I am equally passionate about all my A-level subjects. I won 3rd place in the Jakarta Mathematics Competition 2009 and a Gold Certificate in the UK Individual Senior Mathematics Challenge 2009. The knowledge that I have acquired from Chemistry and Physics has given me an idea to create an all-new concept of a power plant, which utilises the advantages of polymers and nuclear fusion process. Economics has provided me invaluable insight that helps to determine the viability and profitability of a plant by comparing the cost and revenue.

As well as learning, I enjoy tutoring and help other students regularly, specifically in Mathematics, Physics and Chemistry at Bellerbys College. I also became a part-time teaching assistant in a KUMON Mathematics Centre during my high-school breaks in Indonesia. Trying to simplify complicated mathematical questions and to deliver the knowledge to my students is always my highest priority. Education has been a significant part of my life, but I believe that intelligence and talent alone are insufficient for success without discipline and hard work.

Outside my studies, I am active in sports, music, and social organisation. Since Primary School, tennis has been my favourite sport, which is not only about winning and losing, but also about perseverance and consistency. In my quiet time, I play piano and listen to instrumental music, which provides a sense of balance to my mind. I am a member of the UK Indonesian Student Organisation and Vice-President of the Cambridge Branch. In October, we will hold the 2010 International Symposium in London, where topics about Entrepreneurship will be covered. I am on the college newsletter team as a page-layout designer and an article writer, as well as a founding member of the college's student representative committee. One of the events we organised successfully raised £1,000, to help build schools in poor areas of the world via the Building Futures Organisation. As a result of my academic results and my positive contribution to the school, I was awarded the annual Bellerbys College Richard Ryde Scholarship.

I believe that to become a good engineer, I have to be dynamic and adaptable. Engineering is not only about commercial viability and advanced technology, but it is also about ensuring safety and meeting the needs of people in an ever-changing world. With a strong motivation to develop new renewable energy resources, I am looking forward to advancing my knowledge at a top UK university.

Analysis

Kevin conveys clearly his motivation for studying Engineering by linking his interest to his career ambitions. He uses language to show a drive and passion for the subject, and the Personal Statement is well structured since each paragraph follows coherently from the previous. He uses plenty of scientific terminology when describing his work experience to demonstrate his knowledge. He also places good emphasis on his ability to learn in addition to having knowledge of the discipline; an important skill for university studies. In the third paragraph, he demonstrates that he is able to use the knowledge he has gained to create something new, which will impress readers. This Personal Statement lacks slightly in originality and generally uses quite simple language, which means it does not necessarily stand out. However, this simplicity works well in painting a straightforward, honest picture of who the candidate is. He concludes with an insightful ending, showing that he has a mature understanding of the world.

Choo Yan Long (Chemical Engineering)

I have always been interested in how things work. When I was four years old, I had a toy frog that jumped whenever I wound up its springs. I thought that a real frog worked the same way, so I cut open a Bufo fowleri (Scientific name for the common toad). I was rather shocked when brown mush oozed out of the poor frog. Nevertheless, this little incident never dampened my love for science. Fifteen years later, and with a much better understanding of mammalian anatomy, this curiosity has evolved into a more refined intellectual curiosity of how the universe works, and how things work in general. This is why I took up H3 Physics, Essentials of Modern Physics. There is a beauty to just learning about the fundamental laws of physics, trying to understand how things work at the deepest level.

In secondary school, several of my friends and I entered a robotics competition, to design a robot which could maneuver a course using optic tracking devices. It was challenging to construct, program the robot and remove bugs. I learnt that as an engineer, we must be precise and pay attention to detail, because whatever can go wrong will go wrong. I also learnt many valuable technical skills on construction and programming. Perhaps the most important lesson learnt is that engineering and design is complicated, a harmonious blend of many disciples, and there will never be a single 'perfect design'.

I have been fencing for many years, for no other reason than that I love it. After training for three years, I managed to join the national team for Mens' Foil and Mens' Epee. When I graduated from my College (Raffles Junior College), I received the College Colours Award for sports. A reason why I joined fencing is because I found the equipment and technology used in fencing simply fascinating. Electronic fencing combines disciplines ranging from mechanical, electrical and materials engineering. For example, the plastron (A piece of protective equipment used in fencing) is made of cloth reinforced with Kevlar, and can stop a small caliber bullet. Also, the scoring equipment uses complex circuit and logic technology to register hits made. I love fixing, maintaining and fiddling all my fencing equipment, and would often volunteer to help fix my friends' equipment as well.

I have been conscripted into the Singapore Armed Forces for almost year now. I feel that the past year has allowed me to mature and grow tremendously, and to pick up valuable personal, interpersonal and leadership skills. I was posted to be a Military Police Specialist, to be the head of security for an air base. I really enjoyed the technology used in the army, be it a rocket-propelled grenade launcher or a mobile bridge. In my free time, I would find excuses to venture off on my own, just to take a closer look at the fascinating technology used in the army.

I eagerly wait the time when I resume my studies in university. My father is a businessman, and he shares his regrets on how he did not go to university as our family was too poor back then. The dream and responsibility of getting a world-class university education falls on me, and I hope to achieve it. I wish to apply for the engineering course at Cambridge, because I feel that the course is just right for me. Right now I still have a wide range of interests in engineering, and the course at Cambridge allows me to fully explore all these options, allowing me to make a more informed decision in my third year when choosing to specialize.

Analysis

This application clearly embodies genuine fascination for engineering, shown through the fact that the candidate repeatedly links each extra-curricular activity and life experience to the subject, keeping the discussion linked to engineering. By directly connecting military conscription and fencing to engineering, Choo Yan demonstrates passion as well as practical experience. Likewise, the already impressive project of designing a robot is striking as the candidate is explicit about the skills and knowledge acquired. The applicant opens with an amusing anecdote; while memorable, this section could be shortened. Also, the Personal Statement contains a number of grammatical errors, which suggests laziness. Avoid colloquial phrases such as 'back then' or 'how things work' and repeating words in the same line ('curiosity'). The candidate could have cut generic statements such as 'I wish to apply for...', as this applies to every candidate and wastes space. That said, the applicant clearly demonstrates raw enthusiasm, which is vital to interviewers, bolstered by experience which the candidate has made relevant.

Law

James Egan

My desire to study law derives from its diversity, encompassing history, sociology, politics, economics and literature. Its continual development reflects the dilemmas it faces in terms of protecting the rights of the individual against the welfare of society, whilst ensuring equality and justice. An example of which is the right to family life versus child protection, a field in which I am currently working.

My study of history and Ingram's Law: Key Concepts in Philosophy *introduced me to the often debated link between law and morality. Ingram, for example, examined whether Nazi law should be seen as legitimate or 'real law' due to its immoral nature. I was fascinated by the Jurist Carl Schmitt's suggestion that the Nazi regime was more lawful than the anarchic and chaotic Weimar Republic it replaced, after it came to power legally through utilising Article 48 and then created a more stable and ordered society. Is it possible that a dictatorship could be seen as more lawful than the democracy it replaced? This enabled me to research legal positivism which suggests that the link between law and morality is more tenuous. Through my studies of English literature, I became aware of the role literature can play within a legal system by highlighting social injustices which can initiate pressure for change. It also enables us to analyse the impact of law which may be mirrored in the author's fictive world. Of particular interest to me is the role law plays within the economy, protecting both the rights of the consumer whilst also encouraging entrepreneurship and not restricting growth detrimentally; for example, I examined why Standard Oil's monopoly was dissolved to create a more competitive environment for both the consumer and business. Through understanding the context in which law works, we become aware of the dilemmas and controversies it faces and how it continually adapts to meet the changing demands made by society: a more recent example is the controversial debate regarding euthanasia.*

I enjoy reading books about the English legal system; I particularly enjoyed What about Law? *by Barnard, O'Sullivan and Virgo, and Glanville Williams's* Learning the Law *which introduced me to the academic study of law as well as the context in which it works.*

During my gap year, whilst working as an intern in a firm of solicitors, I have been given the opportunity to see the translation of law into its vocation. I have been able to witness law in both the civil and criminal jurisdictions and also research various areas of the law myself. I have also arranged mini-pupillages and marshalling with various Judges where I was able to discuss the controversy of sentencing guidelines and whether the punishments are always reflective of the crime. This, as well as my other previous work experience placements, has only enhanced my desire to study law.

I have enjoyed many leadership opportunities within school, such as being a school monitor, library monitor and co-editor of the history magazine The HISToracle *which furthered my ability to work to strict deadlines and to motivate my peers to participate in extra-curricular academics.*

After I achieved grade eight on the piano, I enjoyed working as a Musical Director and Production Pianist for many amateur dramatic and school productions where I had to create and work to strict deadlines as well as motivating, teaching and leading the actors and adapting the music to suit the needs of the show. Further to this, I have achieved three national medals in water polo, swimming and diving. These hobbies have not only increased my confidence but also developed and enhanced many of the skills necessary for self-discipline and focus needed to successfully complete a law degree.

I am looking forward to the academic challenges that a law degree will present to me and believe it will enable me to pursue my commitment to law into the legal profession.

Analysis

The most impressive thing about this Personal Statement is that it raises mature debates, showing that the student is not afraid to tackle complex ideas within his subject. For instance, the student highlights 'dilemmas', 'immoral' issues and 'controversies' that have affected legal systems, and goes on to show how to address these problems. This Personal Statement shows clearly the aims of the student because he links his desire to study the subject in the context of his career motivations. The candidate draws on evidence and examples to show how he has gone beyond his school material to learn about law. In addition, he includes good analysis of what his hobbies, interests and achievements have taught him. The style of writing is clear and concise. However, the overall structure is at times less coherent; this Personal Statement could do with more connections between the paragraphs to appear more structured. Altogether, the student shows good understanding of his discipline, not only as an academic subject but also in its applications to society as a whole.

Victoria Ting

At a dialogue session, I once asked Singapore's former Attorney-General Prof Walter Woon how he would reconcile having to advance his client's interests with the knowledge of his client's guilt. His reply was simple: a lawyer's allegiance, he said, always lies with the court, and the truth.

This is what so fascinates me about law – the lawyer's responsibility to somehow synthesise an axiom, the Truth, in terms of prescribed guidelines, out of what is always and everywhere rendered in grey. Certainly, I believe the law is structured to capture fairly every notch on the scale of legal responsibility. Yet I also believe that cases like Alan Shadrake's 'contempt of court' charges, and even our drug penalty dichotomising drug addicts and traffickers, all demonstrate that more often than not, the task of the lawyer lies in somewhat impossibly straddling the gaps in the scale, and applying theoretical law to unpredictable reality.

I live in a state famous for its alleged insistence on this black and the white, on the mandatorily condemnable or the perfectly self-righteous. By contrast, I have chosen a course of study (the Humanities) that has taught me to be comfortable with thinking in terms of degrees and uncertainties. Literature and history, for example, studies of the human condition, have cultivated in me skills of critical analysis, of scepticism, of discipline to find and accept nuances in the evidence. More importantly, they have taught me to offer reasoned arguments and rigorously tested conclusions, synthesising facts and precedence. These lessons, I believe, have served me well in my studies so far, and will serve me better in the legal discipline and profession.

Many believe that innocence in capitalist and pragmatic Singapore is a quality to be purchased. This, coupled with the mandatory penalties that many crimes carry, means a source of genuine concern is that many of our underprivileged frequently fall through the gaps. Personally, an acute awareness of the wealth of opportunities I have been blessed with has instilled in me a genuine aspiration to be the kind of lawyer I think they deserve – a lawyer who not only defends, but protects. Thus, I hope to join the Legal Aid Bureau, which ensures equal access to justice and legal representation for the less privileged.

Some may question why I still choose to pursue a career in the public service, which entails having to prosecute, possibly leading to unimaginable consequences under Singapore's severe penal code. I would reconcile this by arguing that an awareness of the flaws of a system is no reason to disengage oneself from it – in fact, I believe we each have a responsibility to approach precisely that which we do not agree with, and earnestly seek constructive change. I will not claim to agree with every facet of Singapore's judiciary or legislation, but I do not wish to be an uninvolved critic either. That is why I hope to study abroad: for the greater emphasis on jurisprudence, advocacy and criminology that it offers, but also for the multitude of perspectives not heard at home that I will be exposed to. I believe my education abroad will not be confined to the classroom, but will start the moment I leave familiar Singapore.

I anticipate the study of law to be the greatest intellectual challenge I will encounter. I believe I will relish this. Yet, I see the strictly cerebral as insufficient motivation. In this, I confess a certain degree of idealism – more than merely the grappling with intellectual abstractions, I'd like to believe the Humanities have taught me, above all, empathy and compassion. At the same session, Prof Woon also commented that the best people did not necessarily make the best lawyers. I hope that my years in university will teach me to be a bit of both. I hope to shoulder this challenge, this privilege, with a humility to learn, a commitment to the truth, and hopefully a wisdom that will come with time. I am more than hopeful; I am excited.

Analysis

We're instantly hooked by Victoria's introductory paragraph – not only does her questioning of Singapore's former Attorney General show an inquisitive and critical mind, but she uses the ex-General's reply to assert a notion that is important to Victoria: a lawyer's allegiance to the truth. Her second paragraph delineates the logistical and ethical dilemmas and contradictions that constantly face lawyers. The main weakness of this Statement is that enthusiasm is not backed up by concrete achievements. Practical attainments – whether they be projects, competitions, or just mentioning books read – are invaluable to admissions committees. Nevertheless, Victoria is clearly a thoughtful student, genuinely fired up by Law in all its complexities and ambiguities. She spends a lot of time analysing not only Law as a discipline, but how legal issues fit into her experiences in Singapore. Her critical faculties are obvious, and her final paragraph reveals a palpable enthusiasm.

Thor Richardson

I am pursuing a world-class education in law because I believe in the benefit of gaining a mutual understanding and appreciation of the legal and business worlds. I will enter law school having earned an Honours in Business Administration from the Richard Ivey School of Business, the top-ranked business school in Canada, along with the 'Investing Potential in Others' award for outstanding leadership and community involvement. A law degree will further my passion for understanding the legal side of business and, more importantly, serve as an invaluable asset to my future aspirations.

I graduated high school from St John's Ravenscourt in Winnipeg with Dean's Honour Roll distinction for exceeding a 90% average. I was recognized for my work and commitment as Community Services Prefect with the Ravenscourt Leadership Award. In addition to managing all of the school's philanthropic programs, I led a number of new initiatives with the United Way to successfully create new programs to help more students impact their communities. I received the J. Taylor Birt Scholarship for respect and commendation from peers and faculty, as well as the Huron National Scholarship for strong academic, community and athletic achievement. I intend to continue this level of achievement in law school.

I was accepted to the International Study Centre in East Sussex to gain experience in other cultures after high school. I was exposed to 16 countries through the program and independent travel. While abroad I was selected as a National Excellence Award Laureate by the Canadian Millennium Foundation.

To further challenge myself, I will complete my degree on exchange to the Lee Kong Chian School of Business in Singapore. I believe that international experience will be increasingly important as the marketplace becomes ever more global. Studying in Asia will allow me to learn amidst one of the most rapidly developing economies in the world.

I have extensive work and leadership experience. I started a delivery and logistics company in 2005 and achieved tremendous success and annual profit growth of over 100% over the past 5 years. I have gained considerable hands-on experience through hiring and managing 6 part-time staff. In 2008, I launched a regional publication by capturing the demand for advertising by Ontario companies to the local market. I have learned many legal lessons, most notably through negotiations to franchise the business model on a profit-sharing basis. In 2006, I was awarded the Albert D. Cohen Scholarship for my entrepreneurial success.

I have greatly improved my leadership abilities in my recent role as President of my section at Ivey. I was able to coordinate and oversee all of the activities of my class and be in constant communication with students and faculty, while still excelling academically. I have learned to effectively manage myself and others – a skill that will serve me well as I take on leadership roles at law school.

Last year I received The Duke of Edinburgh's Gold Award from HRH Prince Edward. The Gold Award is a reflection of my well-rounded achievements and personal strength. I was asked to speak in front of His Royal Highness and reflect on the accomplishment as part of the award events.

My experiences to date have prepared me to excel at a world-renowned law program. I have significant international, leadership and business experience that will add to the diversity of the program and enable me to offer different perspectives. I have received excellent training in case-based problem-solving and have proven my capacity to perform in-depth analysis and logical reasoning to tackle complex problems. Furthermore, I am able to draw conclusions from my analysis and defend my proposition with reason and sound arguments.

The UK has some of the finest law programs worldwide and I am eager to immerse myself in British culture once again. I am confident that I will succeed as a legal and business professional and serve as an international ambassador of my degree.

Analysis

Thor exemplifies impressively high academic performance complemented by broad extra-curricular and unusual entrepreneurial achievement. His hard-hitting facts are direct and his extension of academic interest to non-academic business-related success is particularly outstanding. However, his major flaw is lack of focus on law, sometimes appearing strained to relate his business interests to a law degree. His interviewer will undoubtedly ask why he did not choose to continue down the business path, rather than switching to Law. Likewise, the candidate's striking international focus would be enhanced by an explicit interest in international law. Some descriptions are too vague ('helping students impact their communities') and some sentences are unnecessary ('Cambridge provides a world-class education', and describing interest in British culture). Overall, the application clearly succeeded due to its wide-ranging evidence of dedication, ambition and achievement.

Mathematics and Computer Sciences

Jack Williams (Mathematics)

The first time I remember being interested in mathematical proof was during a discussion about whether 0.999... = 1. In Year 7, I offered a proof based on multiplying 1/3 = 0.333... by 3 but this failed to convince my classmates. From then on, the problem was fiercely debated in maths lessons. It was only in Year 11, after studying geometric series, that I succeeded in convincing the class. By writing 0.999... as a geometric series, I was able to show that the sum to infinity is exactly 1.

This sparked my interest not only in proof, but also in how one person may find a proof convincing or a statement 'obvious' whereas another may not. I came across a similar idea when reading Playing with Infinity *by Rózsa Péter, which discusses different interpretations of Euclid's parallel postulate, each leading to completely different geometries. I wondered whether I would still find the axiom 'obvious' if I had not studied Euclidean geometry from such an early age.*

In Year 7, I took part in the UKMT Junior Maths Challenge and won both a Gold Certificate and Best in School. I found this much more interesting than primary school maths, which had concentrated on arithmetic, as it focused more on logic and geometry. Following this, I was invited to take part in the Senior Maths Challenge, in which I enjoyed exploring challenging, off-syllabus problems, which at first seemed inaccessible but I eventually found novel ways of answering questions which I had not covered in lessons and achieved a Bronze Certificate in Year 8. As I learnt more maths, I was able to answer more of the questions, eventually winning both a Gold and Best in School certificate.

After doing particularly well in the Intermediate Maths Challenge, I qualified for the IMOK Cayley. Focusing more on proof and explanation than simply applying methods, these questions were far more interesting even than the previous round. It is this sort of problem that interests me most and attracts me to a university mathematics course, where ideas can be explored in depth and are not so confined to the exam being prepared for.

In contrast with most maths, which is done independently, the Team Maths challenge gave me the chance to work on problems in a group and share ideas. I enjoyed this rare opportunity in maths and, after winning the local round, we came ninth nationally.

When I left school, I was awarded not only the overall prize for academic success, but also the subject prizes for Maths, Science and ICT, having obtained the highest UMS marks in these subjects and several others. I took AS Maths a year early and averaged 98% in my A-level, with 99% in Core 2 and 100% in Core 1, Mechanics, Core 3 and Core 4. Also, I achieved 100% in Physics and Biology, 95% in Chemistry and GCSE triple Science.

During my ICT course, I ran a support class teaching others how to use Adobe Flash. This developed my communication skills along with the logical and mathematical thinking required for programming.

In October, I am going on a maths week at Villiers Park, where I hope to explore more interesting mathematical ideas and meet like-minded people. I have already attended optional sessions on chaos and fractals at my college so I hope that this week will take these ideas further. These ideas were developed when I read Ian Stewart's Nature's Numbers. *I found the ideas about phase spaces particularly interesting as they provide an elegant solution to a complex problem.*

I began taking piano lessons after leaving school and passed my grade 5 exam the following Christmas. Since then, I have been studying for a diploma and I hope to take this exam soon. As I have to practise for an hour every evening, this has taken considerable dedication and time management. I also developed these skills as managing director for my school's Young Enterprise company, which made a profit from selling memory sticks.

I have read quite a few maths-related books but I particularly enjoyed Peter Higgins' Mathematics for the Curious *and his discussion of probability problems that seemed counter-intuitive. This was because the book presented a question and I was able to solve it myself before reading on to the solution. I found this much more enjoyable than just reading a commentary without actually doing any maths.*

I have recently been volunteering at a local community centre to help Somali children of varying ages with their maths. As some of the students are exceptionally bright, I was asked to provide extension activities for them. This has been challenging as I have had to find simple explanations to more complex problems, testing my understanding of the subject. I feel this has been a worthwhile and rewarding experience for me as well as the students.

Analysis

Jack's opening paragraph seems initially to be a little clichéd – harking back to when he 'first got interested in Maths' – but its strength lies in his specificity. He demonstrates that from an early age he had grasped mathematical concepts, and found different ways to find proofs. Obviously, he has shown a consistent knack for the subject. Moreover, his desire to exceed the requirements for exams, and to pursue more difficult mathematical challenges, is a worthy asset. His other accomplishments are also considerable; he completed his grade 5 in piano within a year of taking up the instrument, while also heading a successful Young Enterprise team. Around all his musical and mathematical commitments, Jack found time to do charity work, demonstrating both his charitable nature and his love for Maths. Jack's closing sentence could definitely be stronger, and the Statement overall is rather long, but his enthusiasm is obvious, and his outstanding ability even more so.

Ben Elliott (Computer Science)

I have long had an infatuation with finding out how things work. Throughout my childhood, I would constantly take things apart with the intention of somehow making them better than they were before. As a result, every room of the house was laden with half-repaired telephones, computers, calculators and anything else that my parents had forgotten to hide from me.

This obsession with technology is what has drawn me to Computer Science, which combines an understanding of how systems work and the theory behind the science while still maintaining a palpable physical aspect – something which many similar disciplines do not offer. Computer Science was the obvious choice for me as it combines the practical aspects of technology with my deep interest in the more theoretical topics I have enjoyed studying in Mathematics. I would love to be able to use rules of logic and reasoning to create real-world solutions for people to use.

The interaction between humans and computers is something I find particularly intriguing, such as the advancements of search engines, speech recognition technology and artificial intelligence. This has led me to begin my Extended Project dissertation on the evolution of our relationship with technology and the ways in which science-fiction authors have speculated on future developments. To date, I have studied Babbage's Difference Engine and the concept of a Turing Machine, together with the works of authors such as Dick, Huxley and Wells.

In order to gain experience of working in a scientific field, I represented my school in the Engineering Education Scheme. The task set for our team was to assess the effect of phase change materials in offsetting the unnecessary waste of energy when heating a building. Our test rig and subsequent report were very successful and our efforts were rewarded with a BA CREST Gold Award. While allowing me to greatly improve upon my teamwork and public-speaking skills, the most valuable experience was to me the application of the sciences in problem solving. My interest in Computer Science was confirmed when I attended a four-day workshop at the University of York. I was introduced to and enjoyed learning the methods of thought and the analytical logic underlying the subject while appreciating the company of others with the same interests as myself. This EDT Headstart course was also very useful in giving me a taste of university life.

In the last year, I have written articles for two different websites concerning recent advancements in software and hardware development for smartphones, tablet computers and other mobile devices. I find the work both interesting and rewarding as I am able to earn a commission while maintaining an in-depth knowledge of progress in the mobile world, which is one of the areas of fastest development. The stunning rate at which ingenious and original applications emerge has illustrated how easy it can be to realise my ideas using the skills obtained from a Computer Science degree.

Extra-curricularly, I have achieved the Duke of Edinburgh's Silver Award and devoted a lot of my time to my school's 'SUSTAIN' environmental-awareness programme. I believe participation in these has expanded my time-management and team-working skills while allowing me to demonstrate my dedication to a cause. Through 'SUSTAIN' I have also been able to contribute to the close community of the school, something which has been very important to me during my time there. To fulfil my interest in languages, I have also been studying beginner's-level Russian and I am currently working towards the Asset Languages Level 2 qualification, alongside my continuation of learning German at A-level.

I would love to learn more of Computer Science and I genuinely feel that I could contribute something myself to the field. By undertaking further education in the subject, I hope to utilise the skills and knowledge I have developed to solve important and unique problems in the real world.

Analysis

Benjamin shows evidence of devotion to the subject, both through school-level projects and by taking an impressive commercial approach to software development, which is regarded as highly employable. His already evident interest in current advances in mobile technology shows ambition, and a long-term plan for the use of his degree. The candidate's comical opening statement is memorable and brief, although the following paragraph is unnecessarily long. Instead, the candidate could expand on his interesting 'extended project', which demonstrates his ability to combine the practical aspects of his subject with an academic and literary background, exemplifying all-roundedness of his understanding of computer science. Elaborating on his 'extended project' would also allow him to further discuss it at interview. The candidate presents impressive engagement with extra-academic study through voluntary courses: his lack of detail about academic achievement is fine as his grades appear elsewhere. Avoid problematic phrases like 'extra-curricularly'.

Julianna Yau (Mathematics)

The Borromean rings, which I first encountered at the 2009 UKMT Team Maths Challenge National Final, led me further into the fascinating world of Mathematics. I have always perceived maths as a subject focused on the manipulation of numbers in order to find solutions. However, as I began to delve deeper, I discovered that it is in fact a far-reaching study, which among other ideas includes the notions of space, structure and pattern. From reading Ian Stewart's Nature's Numbers *and John Haigh's* Taking Chances, *I see that the study of calculus is only the first step on the journey of appreciating maths. Beyond that lies a multitude of disciplines that emerge from the employment of new mathematical discoveries, from the elusive ideas of fractals and chaos, to the complex use of game theory and differential equations in economics. The underlying principles of maths not only intertwine with our daily lives, but also provide insights into the natural world. Stewart's chapter on locomotion links gaits to symmetry and this has illuminated my understanding of groups. Thus I look forward to the inspiring courses on abstract algebra.*

I believe my A-level subjects will enable me to succeed in a course that requires independent and critical thinking. Further Maths demonstrates the importance of a rigorous proof, as contrasted with that of a hypothetical scientific proof. In physics and chemistry, one needs to be curious and resourceful to explore the myriad aspects of science. As a maths scholar at Marymount Secondary School in Hong Kong, I took part in a range of maths events, where I was able to apply learnt knowledge to unfamiliar concepts and connect seemingly unrelated ideas. I achieved 'Distinction' in the Australian Maths Competition, a gold certificate in the UK Maths Challenge and a second place in the regional final of the Team Challenge. These stimulating experiences prompted me to be a maths workshop mentor. Guiding younger mathematicians through problems extended my understanding of maths as I had to explain deeper concepts to them logically. My passion for maths compelled me to continue my pursuit of the study in its various forms. Working as an intern in a finance firm this summer helped me gain hands-on experience in the application of statistics and decision-making techniques in a real business environment. The interdependence between departments showed me that teamwork is vital to the smooth functioning of a corporation. Being the Finance Director of my Young Enterprise company allowed me to put economic theory into practice. Price elasticity of demand taught me to charge consumers accordingly. I am organized and responsible as I have to keep records of our accounts and transactions. I also volunteer as a finance assistant at Barnardo's Charity Shop on a weekly basis, for which I was given the V50 award.

Having been in the school Athletics Team for 4 years, I was privileged to be selected as the Captain, leading and motivating my team to come second in the HK Interschool Athletics Championship. I was also the Chief Editor of the school magazine, supervising my team of reporters to interview professionals of diverse fields, which enhanced my communication skills and the ability to work under pressure. These leadership posts, together with my conscientious academic efforts, earned me a Sir Edward Youde Memorial Fund Scholarship. The perseverance and self-motivation I developed as a keen athlete fuelled me to take up the challenge of the Gold Duke of Edinburgh's Award and the Lifesaver Bronze Medallion. With Diploma level in piano and Grade 5 in singing, I am particularly enthralled by how the laws of maths are incorporated into music and composition to enhance the perception of aesthetic and acoustic beauty. The golden ratio perfectly demonstrates this. It is inevitable that Maths is all around us.

The sheer desire for knowledge and the joy of solving complex puzzles are my drive to continue maths at a higher level.

Analysis

This is an eloquently written Personal Statement. The opening sentence has impact because it opens immediately with mathematical theory. The mention of the 'Borromean rings' could lead to a nice opening question in the interview; by drawing attention to what she knows and is familiar with, the student can almost steer the focus of the interview in this direction. The use of language and style of writing convey a tone that is thoughtful and mature. However, Julianna could have saved some words on what she took away from her A-level choices; it is unlikely to interest the Admission Tutors since other applicants are likely to have taken the same subjects. The student is able to demonstrate social and leadership abilities through previous roles of responsibility, and she goes further to underpin the lessons learnt from her experiences. She then craftily ends the paragraph on her hobbies and interests by relating the presence of Maths to her personal, non-academic interests, reinforcing her understanding of the subject.

Szymon Sidor (Computer Science)

Contemporary civilisation is based on information. Computer Science explores the most important problems concerning this area. I personally believe, that solutions developed during mathematical and technical research are not only crucial to the growth of humanity, but also often amazingly beautiful. Unfortunately to understand the full spectrum of its beauty, the above-average skills are needed. That is why I strongly desire to study Computer Science as my higher education course.

My adventure with informatics began when I was 8. Since then I have had my first computer. I was also given access to the Internet, limited by my parents. Thanks to that when I was 9 I encountered HTML course. I remember that the very same day I created my first HTML page chaotic and without any sense. I was so proud of myself, that I printed the page, and the source code to show my mother how great it is to communicate with PC, so that it understands you.

Since then I have started developing my skills. I have mastered HTML and JavaScript by the end of primary school and PHP by the end of secondary school. Nevertheless, I considered it only as a hobby. Apart from that I did a lot of voluntary work like organising competitions, discos. I finished secondary school with one of the best results and the title of finalist in 3 important competitions (Mathematics, Physics, Chemistry) due to which I gained access to high school in Gdynia one of the best high schools in Poland.

Moving to Gdynia was a complete breakthrough in my life. My school happened to offer the best Computer Science course in Poland. Our teacher found an independent association 'Stowarzyszenie Talent', which helps young gifted teenagers to develop their programming skills, mainly by organising Computer Science camps. Two weeks before my first camp I learned the basics of C++. When I participated in camp's contest for the first time, I was a little frightened by the high level of mathematical skills that tasks required to be solved, but later on it gradually changed. It was on those camps where I first heard phrases like matrix, graph, nimber, interval tree, etc.

I was so bewitched with the new world of unexpected results and beautiful solutions, that I soon managed to catch up with my colleagues from the class who were already familiar with these matters. Learning how computer stores information let me make my solutions even faster, using caching and other techniques. Afterwards I started working voluntarily on camps: creating tasks, lecturing and supervising contests. My achievements were quite satisfying. For example I came 102nd in competition 'Potyczki Algorytmiczne' (Algorithmic Skirmishes), where both students and developers are allowed to participate.

Obviously, as Computer Science cannot exist without Mathematics, I developed my skills also in this area by participating in competitions and reading a lot of literature (Concrete Mathematics, *magazine* Delta, *etc.*).

Due to the distance between home and school I currently live in a dormitory. There I made a few really close friendships. I spend free-time on parties, nearby beach or just hanging out in dormitory. Considering sports I am training acrobatics and running, but not in a professional way. I look optimistically at life, like taking risk, and spontaneous decisions. When it comes to the interpersonal relations I accept different views and beliefs and I hate prejudice.

I adore Computer Science and Mathematics, because of their unexpectedness. Sometimes it is necessary to mix theories to solve a problem. Sometimes it is impossible to get by without inventing completely new theory. Sometimes, results of researches can emerge really surprising, for example high 37% probability in Secretary problem. My goal is to discover similarly unexpected theorem, useful in currently unsolved problems. I strongly believe that studying Computer Science as a higher education course will enable me to achieve it.

Analysis

This application repeatedly displays long-standing and demonstrable enthusiasm for the subject, particularly through the use of exotic language, for example stating that he is 'bewitched' by the 'beauty' of computer science. Raw passion, demonstrated through education, summer camps or extra-curricular activities, is highly desirable to academics wishing to teach you. However, when stating the candidate came 102nd in a competition, he should estimate loosely the number of competitors.

It is clear that the applicant is an international student whose first language is not English: this is by no means a disadvantage, but requires extra caution in various respects. For example, it's advisable to be clear on the distinction between 'high school' and 'secondary school', and to state that his school is top in Poland since British academics will not know the Polish system. It is potentially counterproductive to write that the candidate 'enjoys parties and going to the beach'. This Personal Statement clearly shows that if English is not your first language, it's useful to get an English teacher to check your spelling and grammar, and avoid colloquial phrases. As noted, some courses like Computer Science require candidates to be of a certain 'cultural fit'. Hence some language used in the essay suggests that the student isn't always as clear or as accurate as others in their written communication, and that might suggest that their language skills may not be sufficiently sophisticated for a course like this. Despite this, Szymon's qualities as a potential Computer Scientist clearly impressed the admissions committee.

Humanities

Paula Melendez (History)

Misery in a child's eyes, devoid of hope from witnessing the murder of her family by Colombian guerrilla rebels in the battled countryside of my land of origin; a penetrating look in a destitute mother's face making meals for her children in their smoke-filled mud hut in southern India; hands of children fighting over my used colour pencils when at nine I trekked in an island off the east coast of Africa. It is contact with this present world that has prompted my queries on the role of events, leaders and economic undercurrents in shaping the lives of others. I want to know more: who were the leaders who shaped these conditions? Or was it circumstances rather than individuals that created their situation?

In this respect, studying history has enabled me to examine among other themes – the origins and consequences of the great conflicts of the 20th century. Learning about historiography and its critical influence over historical perceptions has also been key: AJP Taylor's arguments for the outbreak of the First World War, namely political and economic struggles, differed from my reading of Tuchman's The Proud Tower. *Her deep insight into society at the end of the 19th century allowed me to realize that it was not only the leaders of the moment but European society as a whole that set itself on course for a major clash. Although her chapter on the Dreyfus Affair inspired me to write my Extended Essay on the causes of the rise of nationalism in France, I found some of her arguments, especially those on anarchism, to be uncompromising and rather populist in their approach to serious issues that, in my view, may find better treatment in more subtlety.*

Thus I wonder: what does it mean to be a historian in terms of one's personal approach? Language, reason and emotion carry heavy weight in the creation of historical paradigms. Yet, through the ages, these inevitably become obsolete as new evidence emerges, for example Jung Chang's recent reinterpretation of Mao's Long March *breaks the longstanding popular myth of Mao's heroism and leadership in the face of the Nationalists. Hobsbawm's* On History *enlightened me further on how historical paradigms are challenged; namely his belief that the proletariat and economic constraints are the real driving historical forces, contrary to the accepted idea of his time. Although his eloquence garners respect for many of his arguments, I find it difficult to ignore the causal role of Great Men in history, especially when studying the 20th century. Stalin, Hitler, Roosevelt and Churchill undeniably defined the times in which they lived through their charismatic personalities, and yet, as Paul Kennedy recently remarked in the* International Herald Tribune, *'even the most powerful people are constrained by time and space, by geography and history'. And so it was for them too: for all his accomplishments Churchill was unable to prevent the decline of the British Empire, and Hitler's takeover of Europe was stopped short when the USA and the Soviets joined forces to defeat him. The debate of what drives history remains the most intriguing to me as I continue my search for answers.*

Participating in the Student League of Nations, listening to leaders of today, such as Jose Ramos-Horta or Sergio Ramirez, witnessing the vibrant state of affairs of Colombia as well as embracing the cultural and historical richness of my Hispanic heritage and my francophone and Anglo-Saxon education, I realize that history's beauty is its unrelenting contribution to our understanding of human nature, of the functioning of society, a constant and invaluable contribution to resolving today's problems. To me, history is truly the portrayal of humanity's ongoing journey as a continuum of trial and error, of events, moments and personalities; a journey of falls and promptness to magnanimity and truth.

Analysis

Paula's bold, gripping opening paragraph makes her a memorable candidate, but it is a risky approach since it adds little to her credentials and can appear clichéd. Her in-depth critical discussion of various historiographical ideas displays the crucial skills required of history undergraduates, as does her smooth, eloquent and sophisticated language. She shows that she is already aware of key themes and debates in her subject, proving capability to work at an academic level and a willingness to go beyond her necessary studies. Likewise, Paula's breadth of study is commendable, as she is clearly interested and well read across different global, socio-economic historical contexts, complemented by her international background. By contrast, other candidates elaborate on one or two specific interests, but both approaches can be highly effective. Paula's concise concluding paragraph, with minimal discussion of extra-curricular achievements, may strike some readers as unusual, but history tutors are looking for passion and demonstrable interest, so her neglect of extra-curricular successes can do her little harm.

Emma Jones (Geography)

In our dynamic and interdependent modern world, Geography has never been so fascinating, nor so important. As exploding populations, environmental degradation and climatic change threaten our planet, I can see no better time to be studying Geography and gaining an understanding of the processes which shape the complex world we live in.

The relevance of Geography is just one of its great appeals to me. After attending Dr Heaven Crawley's topical lecture 'UK Migration Controversies' at the RGS, I was inspired to read Migration *by Paul Guinness, and was struck by the complexity of this ever-present phenomenon. Another lecture, Lord Stern's 'Blueprint for a Safer Plant', complemented many aspects of my study of 'The Energy Issue' at AS level. This topic was especially engaging, not only for its analysis of links between the successful exploitation of energy and many complex political, social and environmental factors, but also because it allowed me to apply my knowledge to the current energy crisis today in terms of both fossil fuel exhaustion and the need to develop more sustainable technologies in order to combat climate change. The frequent mention of these issues and others in the* Economist *is particularly stimulating as it removes Geography from the classroom and provides evidence of its importance in the modern world. Recently the article 'The Best of All Possible Worlds?' caught my attention as it challenged the view that birth rates fall as countries become richer, altering my perception of global population dynamics. The diversity of fields within Geography is another of its attractions to me. Beyond the A-level curriculum, my interest in population dynamics and civilization inspired me to write a school scholarship essay exploring various theories for the decline of prehistoric civilization on Easter Island and considering its relevance to our future. This project was very satisfying as it revealed a combination of both physical and human issues leading to the collapse, perfectly illustrating the integration of the scientific and the social which is unique to Geography. As an active leader of the School Geography Society last year, I aimed to raise an awareness of the relevance and diversity of Geography by organizing a range of activities, from engaging speakers to topical quizzes.*

A mathematical knowledge of statistics proved invaluable when analysing data gathered on a field trip to the Isle of Wight; a perfect opportunity to apply the classroom theories of ecological succession to reality. My understanding of ecosystems was further enhanced, and my analytical skills tested while completing work experience with the conservation team at Burnham Beeches where I began their 2009 management report based on data which I had collected. Studying A-level French enables me to immerse myself in a different culture and to communicate internationally, a skill which is increasingly important at a time when global co-operation is needed to solve global problems. In my gap year I plan to teach in China before travelling to Nepal and trekking to Everest base camp. Gaining knowledge of Chinese values will further my understanding of China's role in climate-change agreements and enable me to experience a culture very different to my own.

Extra-curricular activities have given me lasting skills beyond those needed for study. I volunteer weekly as a primary school classroom assistant, improving my social skills as well as my patience. I have learnt the importance of teamwork and motivation by participating in the Duke of Edinburgh's Award to Gold level, while my dedication to music has taught me the value of practice, enabling me to achieve Grade 8 in piano and 7 in viola. I enjoy playing in the school orchestra and keep fit by swimming for the school team.

Studying Geography at university can only increase my appreciation of the world and all its processes, stimulating an even greater love for this intriguing, dynamic subject.

Analysis

Emma's Geography application demonstrates the skills all Humanities tutors are looking for: raw passion for the subject, an awareness of academic and global debates and of the real-life implications of the subject, and demonstration of interest and ability. Thus Emma's elaborate discussion of important debates in her field whilst simultaneously making use of literature she has read and talks she has attended make her application strong. Her bold and unambiguous opening sentence also demonstrates her motivation. For Geography applicants, it is advisable to include human and scientific aspects, as Emma does, reinforcing her strength through discussion of field trips and data analysis. Her complementary involvement in her school's geography society is well integrated. Relevant experience is more impressive, so Emma does well to keep her later extra-curricular section brief and straightforward. Likewise, a concise summary of gap-year motivations, plans and aims will suffice. She occasionally uses grammar incorrectly, which should be avoided, especially for essay-based subject applications.

Vincent Yeung (Theology)

Regarded as the 'Queen of all sciences', Theology has shaped the structure of human society. As the foundation of the Western civilization, religion has not only created laws, but also encouraged science. For instance, in the Middle Ages, monasteries were the centres of medical science, just as Daoism was in the East. Having been brought up as a Chinese Catholic, I am familiar with both Christian teachings and Eastern ethics. Although I understand that religion has created a better world by encouraging morality, the question 'does God exist?' has never left me.

In A-level RS, I find the arguments for the existence of God and the Fourth Gospel particularly interesting. Whilst finding Aquinas' five proofs of God's existence logical, Hume's argument of religion, being a man-made remedy for fear and hope, sounds equally plausible. On the issue of the problem of evil, I hold a different viewpoint to the teachings of the Church. Although I agree with St Irenaeus about suffering being the tool for 'soul making', and St Augustine's interpretation of evil as privatio boni, I find it difficult not to doubt Augustine's literal interpretation of Genesis, that all men's sins are due to the fault of Adam and Eve. Instead of privatio boni, Eastern philosophers like Lao Zi took evil as a necessity in order to reflect the goodness, as 'the whole world recognises the good as the good, yet this is only the bad'. Such a cosmic dualistic argument seems more convincing to me. Although Christianity is not a dualist religion, such view could be found in the Fourth Gospel, especially the contrast between light and darkness. I find the symbolic significance of the signs and how Jesus got into conflict with the authorities especially interesting. Jesus of Nazareth by Ratzinger has provided some detailed explanations, while Jesus by Lucas Grollenberge helps the understanding of why Jesus has to suffer even though he is a king.

My interest in Theology and Philosophy led me to enter a Theology essay competition organized by Heythrop College, London, and I was delighted to come second. The title was 'Is the World Charged with the Grandeur of God?' In the essay, I quoted Aquinas and Aristotle on the definition of beauty. I also approached the question from an atheistic aspect. Quoting from Hume, religion began with polytheism, and believers worshipped nature. Therefore the world must be beautiful to such an extent that humans believe it is a creation of the deity. Along with Hume, I quoted Lao Zi as one of my rebuttals against the problem of evil. Towards the end of the essay, I summed up with the traditional Christian idea of love being the true beauty of the world.

As a complement to Theology, I run Lectio Divina groups for juniors in the school. As the Chaplaincy Prefect, I help to ensure that school Masses run smoothly and arrange students to participate in Soup Runs, handing out food to the homeless on a weekly basis. As the leading cadet in CCF, a participant in the 10 Tors Challenge and the Gold Duke of Edinburgh's Award, my leadership skills have been honed, and I have a strong sense of teamwork. As one of the few senior music scholars in the school, I was awarded ATCL on the piano by Trinity College,

London, last summer and distinction in Grade 6 Organ in 2005. As a member of the Student Council, I am used to analysing issues in a critical manner. I have also taken part in the school debating society. As a keen photographer, I have been hired by the school on a number of occasions. I had been highly commended in both the SSF Photography Competition and the International Boarder of the Year Award offered by Hobsons PLC in 2007.

Studying Joyce's A Portrait of the Artist as a Young Man in English A-level no doubt challenges my faith. However, one of the most significant phrases in the Bible – 'Be not afraid' – encourages me to question and understand religion in a more analytical manner, hence wanting to pursue theology to a higher level.

Supplementary

Being brought up as a Catholic in an Eastern tradition, how Christianity blends into other traditions has long been fascinating to me. Christianity and the Transformation of Culture interests me a lot, particularly the way in which Christianity entered China and its impact upon the modern Far East. I would very much like to investigate how the Christian teachings are adapted to traditional philosophy, like Confucianism and Daoism. I have encountered some elements of theories of religion, including Hume's anthropological approach in his Natural History of Religion, Marx's political condemnation of religion and Freud's psychological interpretation, and would love to pursue these aspects further in the Understanding Contemporary Religion paper. I have been introduced to the person of Christ through the Fourth Gospel. I would hope to deepen my insight through the relevant optional paper 'Who is Jesus Christ?'.

Analysis

Starting with 'Theology is regarded as "the Queen of all sciences"...' is a potentially contentious move and needs support, or, at least, a solid defence during the interview. Still, it helps that Vincent has been brought up as a Chinese Catholic, giving him a broader frame of theological or cultural reference. He puts this double-edged knowledge to use by comparing Saints Irenaeus and Augustine with Lao Zi. Vincent makes textual comparisons throughout the Statement, blending them with his own interpretations, showing he is engaged by various texts in different ways, with a capacity for critical thought. This capacity was obviously employed in an essay that came second in a London competition; an achievement that strengthens his application.

Vincent's extra-curricular activities are quite impressive, but don't inhibit the expression of his love for Theology. His concluding paragraph is strong; he admits that his faith has been challenged, but says he overcame it with a mixture of belief and critical thinking. Overall, he seems to be an intelligent, passionate student who holds a personal faith and yet is interested in exploring other religions more deeply.

Jemma Phibbs (History)

I am passionate about history, and since my early years of reading historical novels I have been fascinated to find out more about their wider context. As an A-level student my literature studies of Tennessee Williams have resulted in a desire to find out more about areas of American history such as the Civil Rights Movement and American politics in the post-war era, particularly the differences in Northern and Southern State culture. I am captivated by this period and have enjoyed reading around the subject through Fairclough's Better Day Coming *and Ogbar's* Black Power. *I have a keen and enquiring mind and I am currently researching the impact of black music on the struggle for equality through my EPQ.*

Having recently read Carr's What Is History? *and* Telling Lies about Hitler... *by Richard Evans, my relationship with history as a subject has become more than an interest in a broad span of time periods – which range from the Tudor period to the New Deal policies of 1930s' America. My new awareness of historiography has transformed my view of sources and texts. History now seems to encompass many more dimensions than I could have guessed from studying it at GCSE and A-level. It has led me to pay more attention to the way historians' judgements may be coloured by contemporary and revisionist thinking. Reading much more into the theory of history and how research is conducted has made me realise that a big portion of history is not just learning about the facts of the time period; it is also learning historiography and the many facets of arguments presented by historians and sources of the time. As an extreme example, Irving's case made me incredibly aware of the ease with which historical documents can be manipulated, driven by the desire for recognition or prejudice. Thus I now have a strong desire to learn how to properly research time periods myself, and how to evaluate critically historians' arguments (something I had always rather taken for granted). This is why I would like to take History to university level. Learning about a time period and the events which occurred chronologically seems relatively simple; however, an understanding of the skills which allow historians to develop theories and opinions on the happenings of that time is the part of history I wish to explore in an undergraduate environment.*

I have always worked hard to develop parts of my life other than academia, and I hope to continue this at university alongside a disciplined approach to my studies. This summer I volunteered in the NHS, and was pleased to recently be employed for data entry on Oxford University trials. I have enjoyed the experiences gained from this job – particularly the responsibility of working with confidential patient notes. I also found it interesting to go beyond my work and ask the nurses I share offices with questions about how their research is conducted. I hope that this willingness to work beyond what is required because of personal interest will help me excel in my university course.

I am currently deputy head girl at my school, something I worked hard to achieve that has given me a wealth of experience at activities such as public speaking and helping to organize other students as well as events. I am therefore increasingly articulate in expressing my ideas and well practised at making the best out of every situation with the materials given, which has in turn trained me to work efficiently. I recently organized and ran fundraising for the Haiti aid project for a school in challenging circumstances. Our efforts raised over £1,500.

It was a huge personal achievement and gave me the confidence to volunteer original ideas and the experience of working hard to ensure success of a project. The study of the past is my academic passion; completing an overwhelming project is my personal passion. I believe that my achievements show this, and now I am keen to take them further.

Analysis

Jemma's opening sentence is a bit clichéd but then she quickly demonstrates a real enthusiasm for black American history by mentioning her wider reading and her EPQ. Her mentioning of Carr and Evans shows a conceptual grasp of the practice of history, and the Statement in general gives off a good impression of having read a variety of historical texts. Her reference to her 'new awareness of historiography' indicates her capacity to absorb new concepts, a valuable skill for a historian. Moreover, she is specific as to why she wants to study History at university level – she wishes to study primary sources in depth. Such enthusiasm, mixed with an awareness of the limitations of historians, makes her a strong candidate. Her extra-curricular activities seem interesting and indicative of initiative, and she ends with a clever touch – a melding of personal and academic passions that shows she is neither a workaholic nor a slacker.

Rumen Cholakov (History)

Two grumpy old men, a diplomat and a historian – that was the beginning of my journey into history and my early inspiration. Throughout my childhood I often went along with my grandfather to meet his best friend, Professor Andrei Pantev. Once we discussed the Bulgarian Liberation. While I was focused on its Russian support, he revealed to me the role of Britain and Western public opinion. I went on to look at Ann Pottinger Saab's Reluctant Icon *and observed how support in Britain gathered momentum. Despite being detached from events in Eastern Europe, the Bulgarian Agitation still managed to affect foreign and domestic politics. Studying Britain to understand the past of Bulgaria, I was intrigued with how national events can have an international impact.*

I also became interested in what causes revolutions. 'There was no republican thought in 1642'; I was struck by the words of Dr David Smith in his lecture on Charles I as they showed how quickly popular movements can radicalise. Napoleon and Hitler: A Comparative Biography *by Desmond Seward exemplified how this process has then lead to dictatorships, but did not entirely convince me that studying those individual cases can prevent the rise of new national 'saviours'. Dictators are born from a state of crisis when collective behaviour is hardly predictable. Napoleon and Hitler lived in different epochs and such comparisons are problematic because they tend to overlook the particularity of each case.*

I entered the Trinity College Robson History Prize and my essay on 'Why Was There a Thirty Years War?' was highly commended. S. H. Steinberg's The Thirty Years War and the Conflict for European Hegemony 1600–1660 *showed the interrelation of politics and religion in the causation of the event and I decided to invent the concept of 'politigion' to illustrate the inseparable connection between them at the time. Indeed, politics determined the motives of the major participants such as Sweden and France, but were mostly interlinked with and justified by religious causes. The war between two Catholic states that followed is thus ironic, but understandable.*

My historical education in Bulgaria was focused around studying European history in breadth. Since taking IB History in the UK, I have seen the value of detailed study. I read J. A. Sharpe's Early Modern England: A Social History 1550–1760 *and admired his use of different social sciences to understand historical issues. Studying demographics provides a basis for comprehending London's industrial growth, which was a main factor contributing to Parliament's military and political victory in the Civil Wars. In a similar way, I find that studying English Literature and Economics helps me to understand the past.*

My extra-curricular activities are also widely linked to history. When becoming the English Speaking Union's International Public Speaking Competition finalist and IDEA World Debating Champion and Best Speaker, I tried to incorporate historical examples into my arguments and explore their consequences in contemporary affairs on topics such as 'Censoring Expression that Promotes Violence is Just'. As President of the Whitgift History Society, I worked with my classmates on projects including a simulation of the French Revolution and an exhibition of HMS Mary Rose *hosted at my school and chaired talks by Professor Janet Hartley and Dr David Smith.*

An international scholar in England, I left my country to broaden my cultural experience and learn how to deal with the everyday necessities of an independent student life. The enormous diversity of the two societies in which I have lived has led me to consider what has made them so different and how the histories of and relationships between states have shaped the world as it is today. I am driven to ask 'Why?' and I feel I must pursue the opportunity to answer this question at university.

Analysis

This Personal Statement has an interesting, gripping introduction which is personal and gives an effective overview of who the candidate is. Throughout the Personal Statement, Rumen makes interesting references to his personal background, which makes this Statement more memorable. He includes good examples of readings to show his commitment to studying and researching the discipline. In the third paragraph, the student offers some of his own views on certain historical issues, which first of all shows his ability to analyse what he has learnt, and secondly could provide a convenient point of discussion in the interview. Further, Rumen ties his extra-curricular interests closely to his passion for his subject. He concludes with an interesting ending, but the points made in the conclusion with regards to his motivation for wanting to study History could come earlier on in the Personal Statement. It also offers a different explanation for his motivation than that in the introduction, making it unclear which of the two is actually his prime motivation.

Frazer Watt (Philosophy)

I assure you that I would be recounting some sort of heartwarming childhood anecdote of the epiphanic moment in which I was struck by a passion for philosophy, but the truth is, I only discovered it a year ago. And, rather mundanely, it happened over a couple of weeks in a classroom. Despite always having a philosophical disposition, in that I have always liked the 'big questions', I feel fortunate to be writing this statement, as I almost did not pick up philosophy at AS-level, and if I hadn't, right now I would probably be an indifferently dispassionate language applicant.

I feel like Philosophy, and the study of it, has genuinely improved my life. I love how my new understanding of certain concepts illuminates my experience and adds new levels to it, often ridding me of common misconceptions or lack of awareness – I now know whether a tree that falls in the woods when nobody is around to hear it makes a sound. So I strive to understand more, not only out of a fundamental desire for self-improvement, but increasingly out of pure hedonism.

However, the question still remains, why should you accept me over all the other applicants? I hope I have managed to adequately convey my passion for the subject. Unfortunately, it's up to you whether you believe me or not, as anyone – passionate or not – could have written the same, or even copied me. I have only one, Wittgensteinian, response, that it would be impossible to do your job constantly doubting the validity of the emotions expressed in these statements. In the same way you wouldn't just walk past a friend who lay on the ground acting in severe pain because they may be faking, you cannot doubt my passion. If you could, the emotional, personal aspect of all statements would be equal and thus drop out of contention, rendering the statements themselves irrelevant. Why would you be wasting your time reading this?

I believe we are both in need of each other. I want to go to your university, because it is a top university, and is respected by employers. However, it is so respected and has such a high reputation because of the quality of graduate it produces. You want to accept, understandably, the most talented of students, so that you can let them prosper and become of this highest quality. This is where I believe the process reveals a very circular nature. I want to go to your university because of its reputation; you want me because I can develop and give you the reputation that makes you so respected. This is, of course, presupposing that I am one of the talented students that you are looking for – the very thing I am trying to convince you of here.

In order to stand out, although it seems I am already trying to do so by being so self-referential, as this seems the necessary thing to do, I will refrain from going into tedious detail about my trite achievements, like the fact that I achieved grade four in electric guitar or worked as a range assistant at a golf driving range, and how they supposedly make me so suited to study your course at your university. Instead, I should tell you other, relevant things that you can't learn from my predicted grades or exam results. Except for my time at sixth form college, I have spent the whole of my education at public schools, culminating in three years at Charterhouse. I left Charterhouse mainly out of boredom and dislike of the boarding system, but have only begun to realise that I now consider leaving as one of the best decisions of my life. I have proven to myself that I am a competent independent worker. I hated the structure of the timetable at Charterhouse, and now relish my freedom to choose when and how much I work. Consequently, a new maturity developed: I now understand that despite whatever pressure a school, peer, parent or superior may put on you, ultimately performance solely comes down to you, and you are wholly responsible. This is why I trust myself to prosper and profit from the autonomous university education style.

Analysis

If you're looking for an example of a memorable Personal Statement which stands out, then this is the one. The student uses the second person and a conversational tone to directly address the reader and demand attention. He opens with an attempt to come across as an honest applicant and dispel any bold claims of how the subject has always been rooted in his nature – which is what most Personal Statements try to demonstrate. This unconventional, dismissive tone continues throughout the Statement, creating a fresh approach for the reader. However, this should be considered a 'high-risk' strategy – the reader may like it for its originality, or they may see this as arrogant or unreliable in its deliberate avoidance of justification and hard evidence. In this particular case, it worked, perhaps because this is a Personal Statement for a subject which by nature encourages originality of thought, but also because the candidate has managed to include evidence of his understanding of the subject. For instance, the paragraph posing the question of why the reader should accept this applicant is grounded in philosophical argument that is both coherent and logical.

About the Editors

Warren Zhang – Chief Editor, Content and Analysis

Warren is an Australian-Chinese living in Australia. He holds a Bachelor of Economics from the University of New South Wales, and he has an MBA from Cambridge University. He has more than five years of financial services experience working for KPMG, Goldman Sachs and HSBC in Australia and Hong Kong. He is also an Australian surf lifesaver with Surf Lifesaving Australia.

Hemant Mohapatra – Chief Editor, Content and Analysis

Hemant Mohapatra holds an MBA from Cambridge University and currently works in Google's Business Development team in Mountain View, USA. Winner of several international literary awards, Hemant was recently selected as one of the top 50 emerging poets in the world by University of Virginia Press. The anthology, *50 Best New Poets 2011*, was released worldwide in January 2012. Hemant has one US patent (pending) and has co-authored one conference paper.

Anna Claeys – Co-Editor, Analysis

Anna Claeys is a third-year History undergraduate at King's College, Cambridge, and a student journalist and writer. Prior to university she achieved the top mark in her year in the International Baccalaureate in London, writing her Extended Essay on the Cambodian genocide, an unusual topic which she thinks won her a place at Cambridge. She is an avid traveller and also took a gap year.

Arjun Sajip – Co-Editor, Analysis

Arjun Sajip is a second-year Historian at Downing College, Cambridge. Within the field, his particular interests have included early American history, cultural history in eighteenth- and nineteenth-century Europe, and depictions of memories of the Second World War in French cinema. He has edited several sections of *The Cambridge Student*, the weekly student newspaper, and contributes regularly to various sections. He is passionate about music and cinema, and loves literature.

Gwen Jing – Co-Editor, Analysis

Gwen Jing is an Economics student at Murray Edwards College, Cambridge. She was born in China and grew up in the Netherlands before attending secondary school in Harpenden, Hertfordshire, where she currently lives. She is News Editor for *The Cambridge Student* newspaper and has a passion for music, tennis and travelling.